Moods In Wire™

A Comprehensive Guide
to the Fine Art
of Wirewrapping

VOLUME 1

Ellsworth "Ed" Sinclair

Published by E.E. Sinclair
P.O. Box 2011
Manassas, VA 22110

ISBN 0-9640483-0-2

Library of Congress Catalog
Number 94-94275

Published in the U.S.A.

First printing 1990

Second printing 1994

Art Direction & Design:
LaVonne Kaseman, Denver, CO

Photography:
James L. Digby, Loveland, CO

Computer Illustrations:
William W. Ivers, Denver, CO

Typesetting:
Candace Harron, Denver, CO

Ellsworth "Ed" Sinclair

Ed Sinclair

A man of diverse interests, Ed Sinclair studied drama at the Shakespearean Institute at Stratford on Avon in 1959, and followed that in 1962 with a two-year stint with the Peace Corps in Liberia, West Africa, where he "taught a little bit of everything, including history, literature, and carpentry." He recently retired from a twenty-five year teaching career in Fairfax County, Virginia. Ed Sinclair is a graduate of the University of East Carolina and the University of Virginia.

As a native Virginian, he has spent many hours pursuing his mineral collecting hobby throughout the state. Early experiences involved being Field Trip Chairman (and later President) of the Mineralogical Society of the District of Columbia. He is currently a member of the Woodbridge Mineral Club and the Northern Virginia Mineral Club. He still collects when time permits. His interest in minerals led him to frequent the gem and mineral shows where he was introduced to wirewrapping. After a short 10 hour course and a year of practice, he embarked upon the craft show circuit in the mid 1970's, doing craft shows from Gettysburg, Pennsylvania to Ashville, North Carolina. Also at that time he served two terms as President of the Northern Virginia Handcrafters Guild, of which he is still an active member.

Ed lives in Manassas with his wife and son, and spends many weekends on the craft show circuit. Future plans include retiring to the Shennandoah Valley near Harrisonburg.

Preface

Wirewrapping is a widely practiced art. Many systems are employed by many wirewrappers. Expressed in this book are original systems of my own, plus variations of systems I have seen or learned.

It is not my intention in this book to copy, duplicate, plagiarize, or infringe upon any existing copyrighted material. Any resemblance to such an intent is purely coincidental and unintentional.

Dedication

This book is dedicated to my wife Phyllis, whose encouragement led me to the wonderful world of wirewrapping.

This book is also dedicated to my wirewrap instructor, Dan Pompa of Burtonsville, Maryland. His talent and his book inspired the pages that follow.

This book is further dedicated to all of those individuals who aspire to do something different. If you have chosen wirewrapping, then you too are as unique as this fine art. Go to it!!! Good luck and have fun!!!

Table of Contents

Introduction 9

Chapter One: Basic Tools for Wirewrapping
#1 Equipment 11

Chapter Two: Materials
#1 Wire 15
#2 Stones 15
#3 Miscellaneous 16

Chapter Three: Wire Rings
#1 Simple Wire Ring 19
#2 Swirl Wire Ring 21
#3 Double Loop Love Knot Ring 22
#4 Fancy Swirl Loop Ring 24
#5 Scrambled Wire Ring 25
#6 Plain Bead Ring 26
#7 Fancy Bead Ring 28
#8 Multi-Bead Ring 28
#9 Modified Bead Ring 29
#10 Simple Free Form Ring 30
#11 Fancy Free Form Ring 39
#12 Free Form Shark's Tooth Ring 41
#13 Standard Form Ring 42
Chart for Wrapwires 47

Chapter Four: Bracelets
#1 Simple Wire Bracelet: Three Wire Braided 49
#2 Standard Form Bracelet 56

Chapter Five: Earrings
#1 Bird Cage Earrings 59
#2 Earring Variations 62

Chapter Six: Pendants
#1 Single Wire Pendant 63
#2 Three Wire Pendant 68
#3 "Classic Pendant" 73
#4 Plain All Wire Pendant 77

Chapter Seven: Stickpins

#1 Bird Nest Bead Stickpins 79
#2 Bead Stickpin 82

Chapter Eight: Sharks' Teeth

#1 Small Shark's Tooth with a Single Wire 85
#2 Large Shark's Tooth (3" - 5") 88

Chapter Nine: Spider Pins / Webs

#1 The Spider Body 95
#2 Spider Legs 101
#3 Spider Web 102

Chapter Ten: Crosses

#1 Cross 107

Chapter Eleven

Epilogue 111

Introduction

Welcome to the wonderful world of wirewrapping. You will discover in a very short time many facets of this unique art, and in turn, you will also discover many hidden facets of your own personality and talent.

Wirewrapping is one of the most unique means of creative self expression. Every personality is as different as fingerprints. Every wirewrapper has a different "personality print" which is reflected in his work.

In the pages that follow, I have simply shown my own approach to wirewrapping. There are many things that other wirewrappers do that I don't, and vice-versa. This book is by no means the last word in wirewrapping. This is my attempt to pass on to you my own ideas and experiences, and to relate what has worked well for me.

There is not, to my knowledge, a comprehensive wirewrap book on the market today. This book is my effort to fill that void. Each chapter has been carefully thought out and organized into step by step, illustrated instructions on how and what to do.

It is appropriate at this time to offer a bit of advice derived from experience:

- When wrapping, do not rush. If you are in a hurry to get finished, then wirewrapping is not for you.
- **PATIENCE, PERSEVERANCE, AND PRACTICE IS THE NAME OF THE GAME.** It is absolutely imperative to do your homework. At least one wrap a day will help you develop the necessary feel for the wire and will help to keep the fingers nimble. Do not be too critical. Do not contemplate a piece too long. "Learn to do by doing and doing...and doing...and doing. Above all, don't ever give up...persevere!"

- All the talent and skill in the world becomes meaningless if you work with inferior materials, particularly with cut stones that are of poor quality. Using top quality stones means spending a little more money, but in the long run, you have a finished product of exceptional beauty. Inferior stones, no matter how well wrapped, will still reflect their inferiority.
- Don't ever give up on a wrap no matter how bad it looks or if a wire breaks. Some of my best designs have as their origin a messed-up wrap or a broken wire. Remember, **PATIENCE, PERSEVERANCE, AND PRACTICE IS THE NAME OF THE GAME!**
- Wirewrap jewelry should reflect a distinctive delicate look; after all, wire is delicate. To strive for any other look is contrary to the nature of the wire and the concept of wirewrapping.
- Wirewrapping is like opening a door to one's imagination. The possibilities are astoundingly infinite. Be willing to accept any challenge. Walk that path not often traveled before. Dare to be different and you too will be a "happy wrapper."

- Remember: **PATIENCE, PERSEVERANCE, AND PRACTICE IS THE NAME OF THE GAME.**

Instructions are written for right-handed people; if you are left-handed, please reverse the instructions accordingly.

#1 EQUIPMENT

Pliers: All pliers should be the 4" size.

Chain Nose Pliers: These pliers are similar to the tapered needle nose pliers except these pliers have a flat surface on the inside of the jaws. These pliers are used to tuck in ends of wires. They provide a real good grip to forcefully handle the wire without scratching it. They are also used to force the end of the wire through extremely tight places.

Wide Nose Pliers: The pliers are used to bend over ends of wrap wires, crimp ends together, hold wires while bending, straighten bent wires, flatten wire, and hold groups of wires flat.

Needle Nose Pliers: These pliers are similar to the chain nose pliers except these are tapered a little more and have no flat surface to grip the wire. These pliers are used to make various sizes of loops. They can also be used to tuck in ends and are very useful when making earrings.

Side Cutters: Used for cutting the wire.

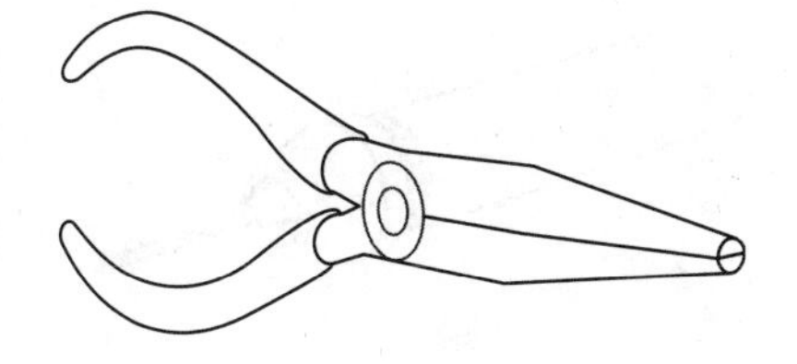

Chain Nose Pliers

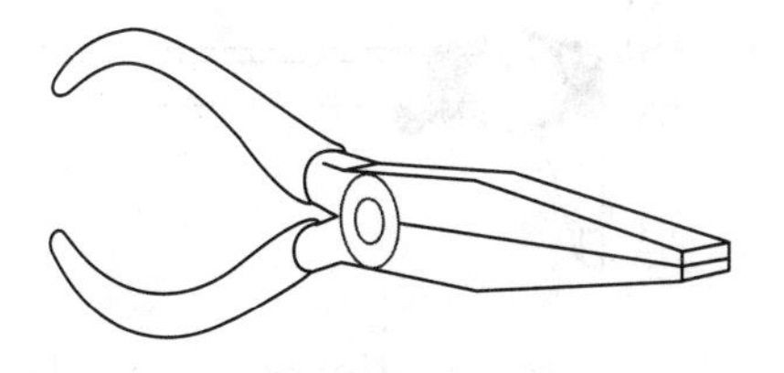

Wide Nose Pliers

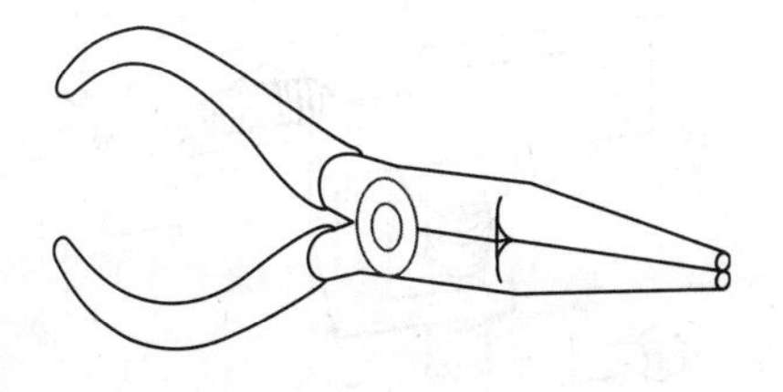

Needle Nose Pliers

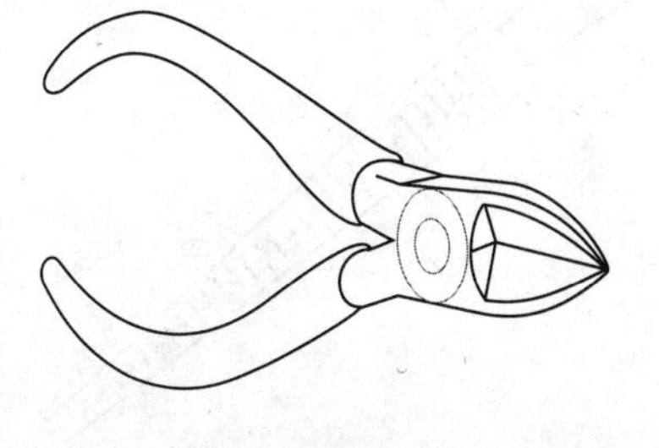

Side Cutters

BASIC TOOLS FOR WIREWRAPPING

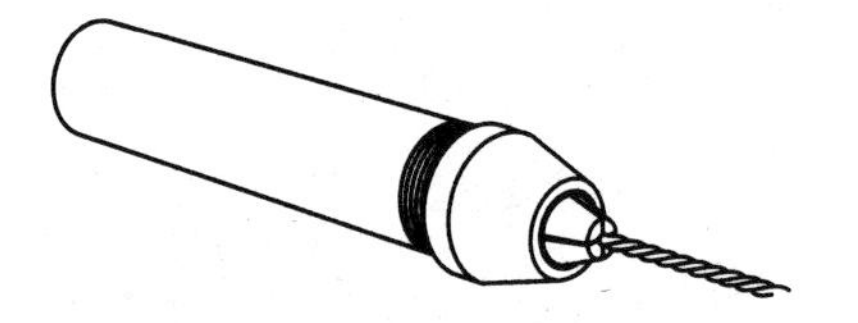

Pin Vise

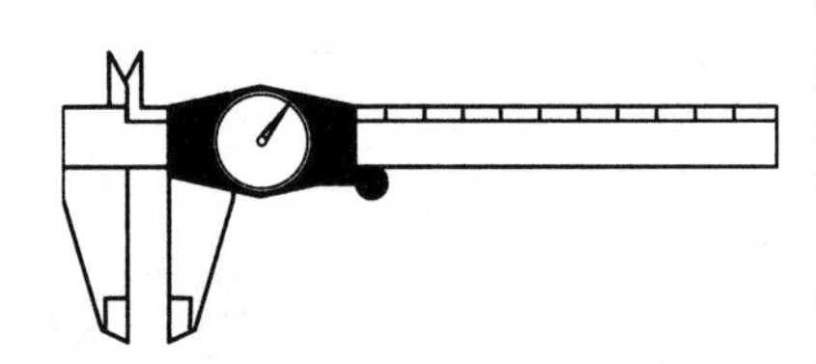

Calipers

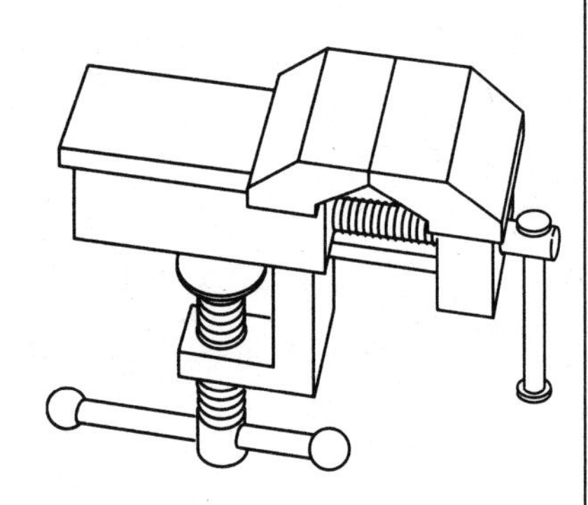

Jeweler's Vise

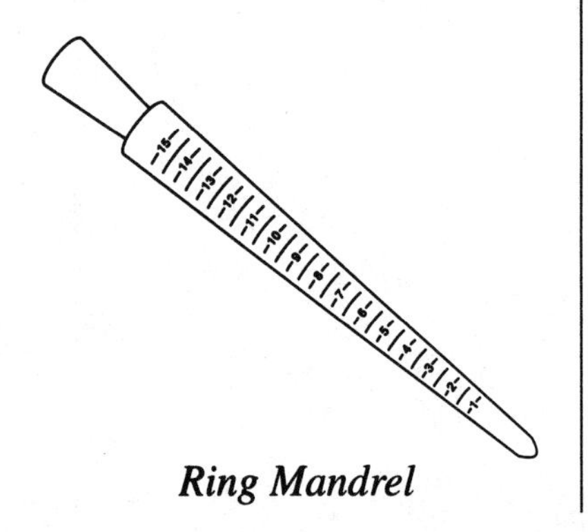

Ring Mandrel

Pin Vise: Used for twisting wire. It is adjustable to all sizes of wire. The wire is passed through the vise. Tighten the vise on the wire tight enough to still slide it. Make sure the end of the wire nearest the head of the vise is held securely. Tug gently on the vise as you twist it. Take no more than 1/4" - 1/2" bites. The number of twists will determine of you have a fine or coarse pattern. **IT IS IMPORTANT TO REMEMBER THAT TOO MANY TWISTS CAN BREAK THE WIRE.**

Calipers: Used to measure the size of stones for rings (so wrap wires can be accurately placed.)

Jeweler's Vise: A very small bench vise 4" or smaller is used in making bracelets and other jobs you will discover.

Ring Mandrel: (Grooved or ungrooved) Used for sizing rings.

18" Steel Ruler: (Corked back) Used for measuring wire and finding other measurements.

Small Pocket Knife: (With pointed blade) Point is used to create small openings for wire to be forced through.

Jeweler's File: For filing down rough edges of cut wire.

Opti-Visor: For magnification -- especially when making free form rings.

Ring Sizer Set: For measuring fingers. **MAKE SURE THE RING SIZES ARE CALIBRATED WITH THE RING MANDREL.**

Plastic or Leather Hammer: Used for shaping rings on the mandrel and making bracelets.

Compartmental Box: (Wood, plastic, or metal) For storing odds and ends. Should be at least 12" x 12" with eight to ten compartments.

Ring Sizer Set

#1 WIRE

A. Wire for Finished Jewelry:

14kt. 1/20 Gold filled. Full Hard. Round and Square:

20 gauge .032

21 gauge .028

22 gauge .025

Sterling Silver. Full Hard Round and Square:

Same gauges as listed for gold.

B. Wire for Practice:

Brass Wire - Square 21 gauge (.028)

Copper Wire - Square 21 gauge (.028)

#2 STONES

A. Assortment of beads: 4mm to 9mm

B. Assortment of baroque stones tumbled and polished

C. Assortment of polished slabs, 1" to 3" in size

D. Assortment of cabochons, oval, marque, round, oblong, free forms, 12mm x 10mm to 30mm x 40mm in size

E. Assortment of fossilized sharks teeth, 1/2" to 3" in size

#3 MISCELLANEOUS

A. Jewelers cloth

B. Piece of felt to cover work area

C. Small work table: 30" x 18" x 12"

D. Two small plastic boxes for scrap wire: 3" x 5" x 3" with lid (one for gold and one for silver wire scraps)

E. One fine line black felt tip pen for marking places for wrap wire placements.

F. One small roll of 1/2" surgical cloth tape.

G. Cotton draw string bags to keep wire in.

H. Two small carrying cases to store wire and tools.

WIRE RINGS

The variety of wire rings is infinite. Their attractiveness is dictated by the design in relation to the type of wire used.

It is important, as in all wirewrapping, to maintain that delicate look; therefore, I do not use 20 gauge wire in any **ALL-WIRE** rings except for the Double Loop Love Knot ring.

For bead rings I prefer to use 21 gauge (.028) round wire for 6mm beads. For larger beads I prefer to use 20 gauge (.032) wire. I do not recommend 22 gauge (.025) wire for bead rings; 20 gauge wire is fine, but more difficult to work with.

For the Plain and Fancy Free Form rings I use 21 gauge square wire exclusively for sizes 6 or smaller (20 gauge can be used, but it is simply my choice to use 21 gauge). Every wire-wrapper is different, so experiment.

For all Standard Form rings above a size 4, I use 20 gauge square wire exclusively.

I have a name for every style of ring I make, and throughout this book I will refer to those rings by name. Please refer to the illustrations on the following page for a visual explanation of each.

ILLUSTRATION OF RING TERMS

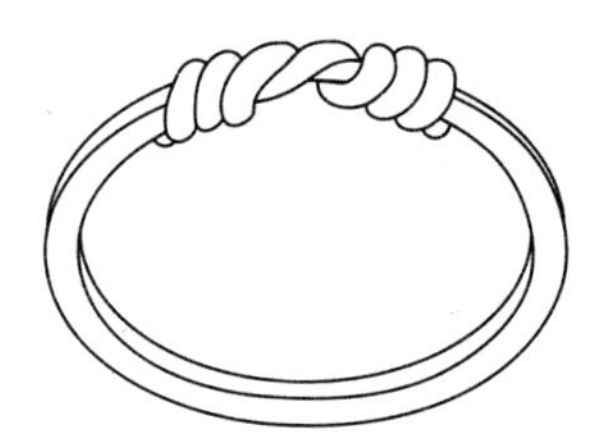

Simple Wire Ring

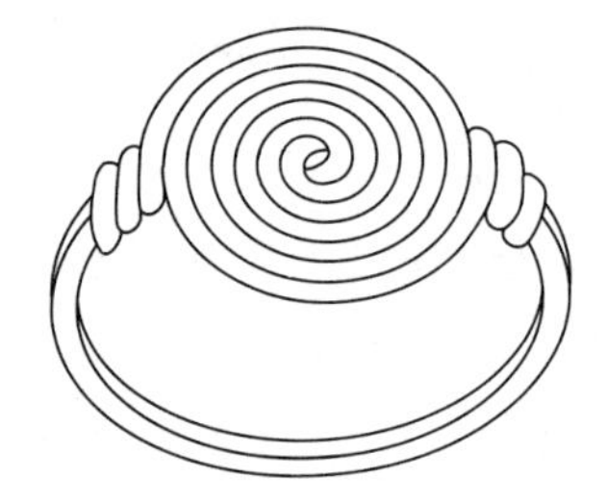

Swirl (Wire) Ring

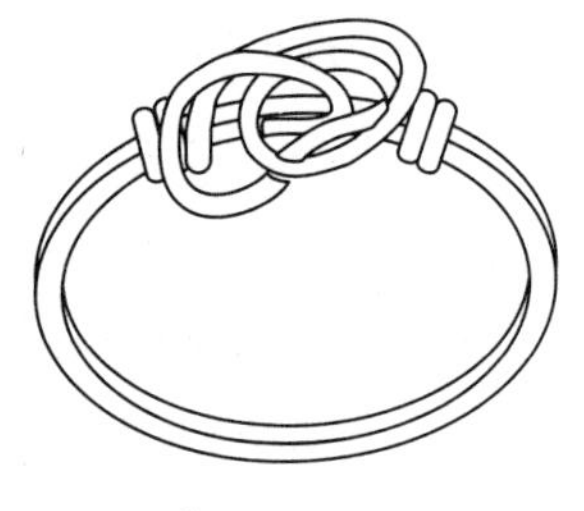

Double Loop Love Knot

Fancy Swirl Loop Ring

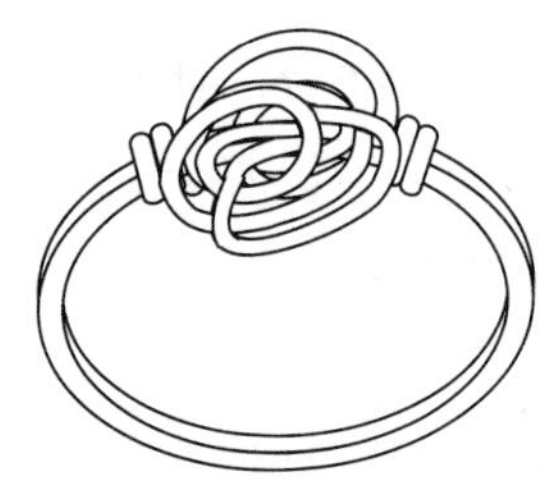

Scrambled Wire Ring

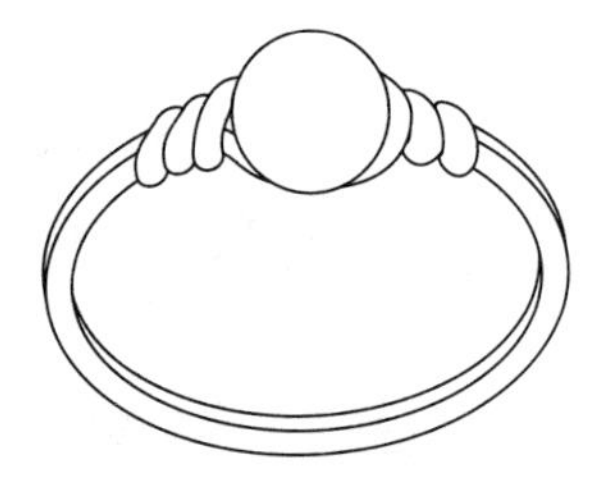

Plain Bead Ring

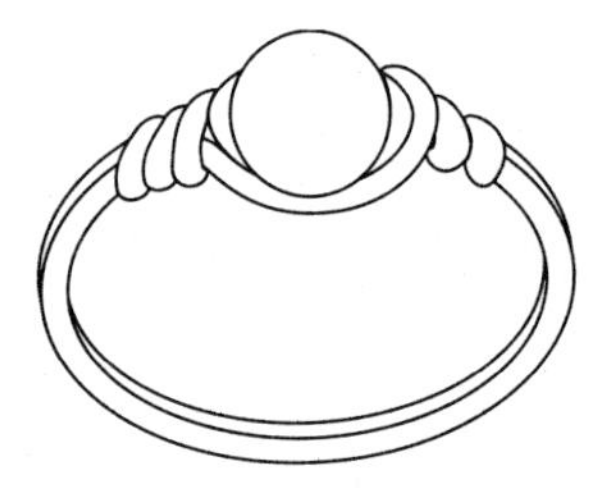

Fancy Bead Ring

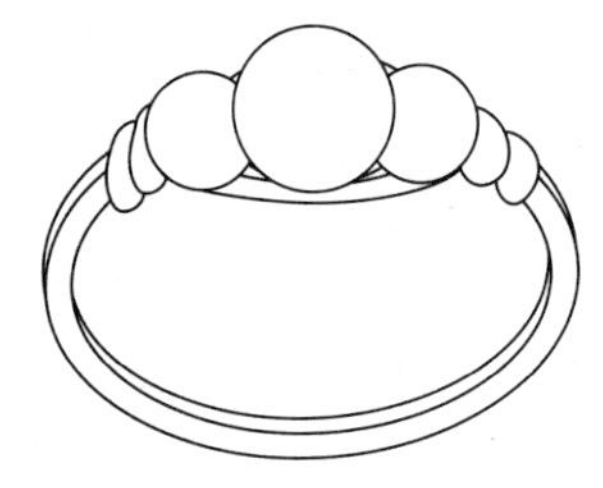

Multi-Bead Ring

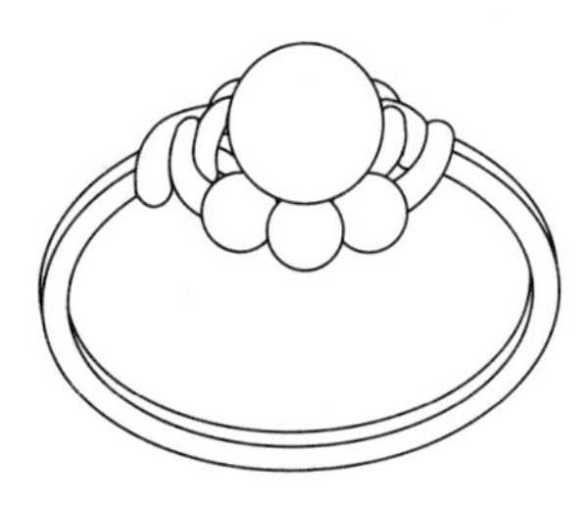

Modified Bead Ring

See photo insert for the rings shown above and also for the Simple Free Form Ring, Fancy Free Form Ring, Free Form Shark's Tooth Ring, and Standard Form Ring.

#1 SIMPLE WIRE RING

A. Cut a piece of 21 gauge round wire, 8" long.

B. Place center of wire on the ring mandrel one size smaller than intended size. (If you have strong fingers and can hold the wire tight against the mandrel, then bend wire around mandrel on the intended size, not one size smaller.

C. Wrap the wire twice around the mandrel so that the ends are of equal distance from center of mandrel. Make sure the wires going around the mandrel are not crossed the second time around. *Diagram 1*

D. Hold the wire against the mandrel very tightly with thumb and forefinger of the right hand. Bend wire as shown in *Diagram 2.*

E. Continue to bring the ends around in opposite directions (hold the wire tight up against the mandrel) until the wires are at opposing 30 degree angles as seen by the dotted lines in *Diagram 2.*

F. Now slip the ring off the mandrel. Hold it with the wide nose pliers on one side as indicated in *Diagram 3.*

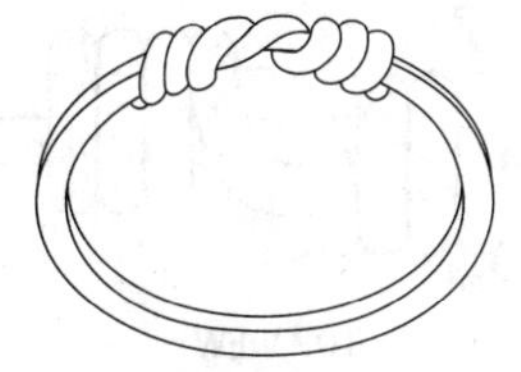

Simple Wire Ring

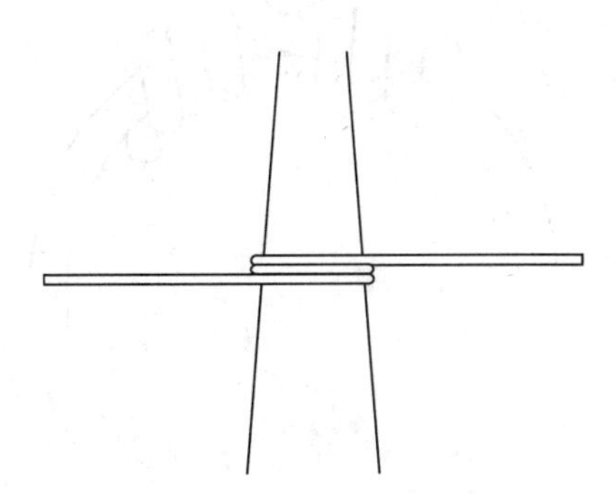

Diagram 1

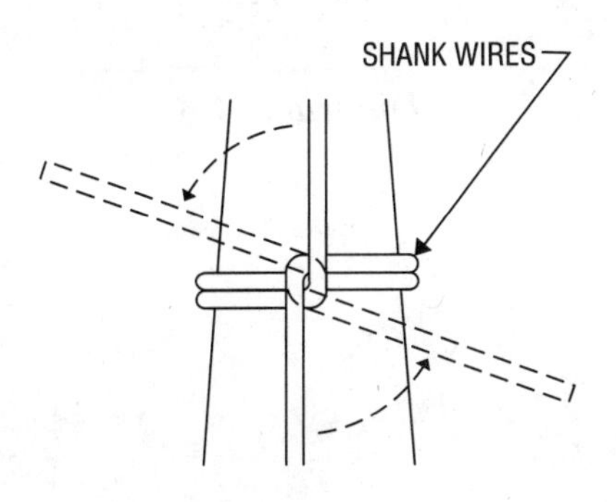

Diagram 2

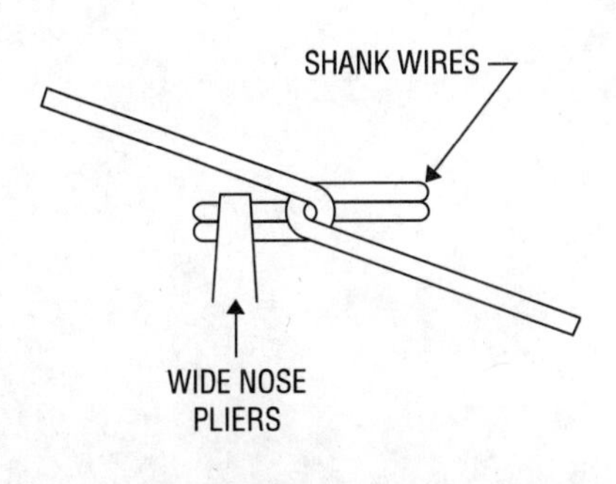

Diagram 3

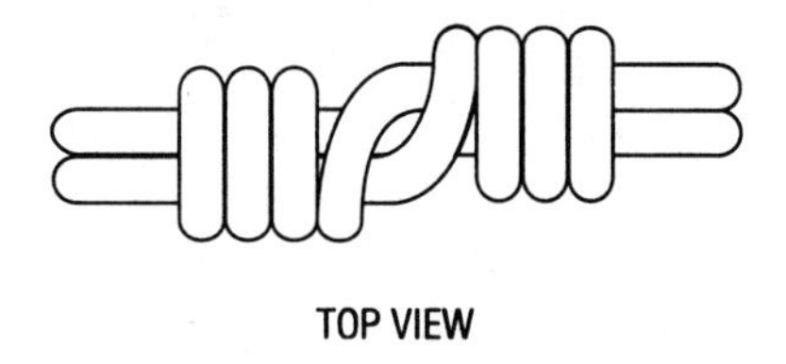
TOP VIEW

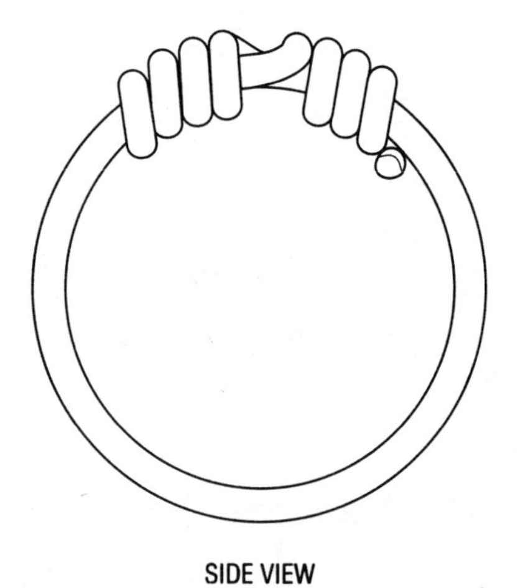
SIDE VIEW

Diagrams 4 & 5

G. Wrap ends of the wire three times around the shank wires at the top of the ring, one side at a time. Be sure to make the wraps very close to each other and on a slant. The chain nose pliers can be used to do the wrapping.

H. Make 3 to 4 wraps on each side, then cut off wire ends at an angle as close to shank wires as possible (on top). *Diagrams 4 & 5*

I. Put the ring back on the mandrel and tap it gently with plastic hammer.

Also check the size. If it is smaller than the intended size, then next time begin to bend the wire around the intended size instead of one size smaller. If the ring is larger than the intended size, then you must hold the wire tighter to prevent it from slipping during the initial wrap or begin with a smaller size.

This ring can be stretched one-half size larger if necessary.

#2 SWIRL WIRE RING

A. Follow Steps A through E as you would for the wire ring except do not stop at opposing 30 degree angles. Make a pin wheel design by continuing to bend wires in flat circular pattern around each other using chain nose pliers to hold it flat until you have a design like *Diagram 6*:

B. There is no special size for the swirl. I have found small swirls are more popular.

C. Wrap wires should be in opposite directions so they can be wrapped tight and close to swirl on opposite sides. Cut them off at angle, put ring on mandrel and tap into shape. (This ring done in twisted wire looks twice as good as it does in plain wire.)

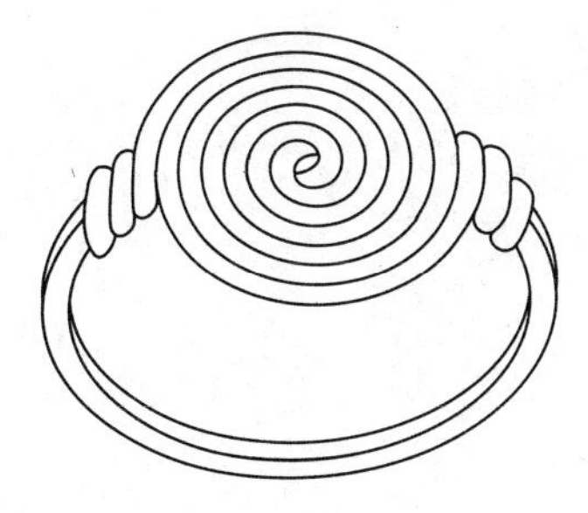

Swirl Wire Ring

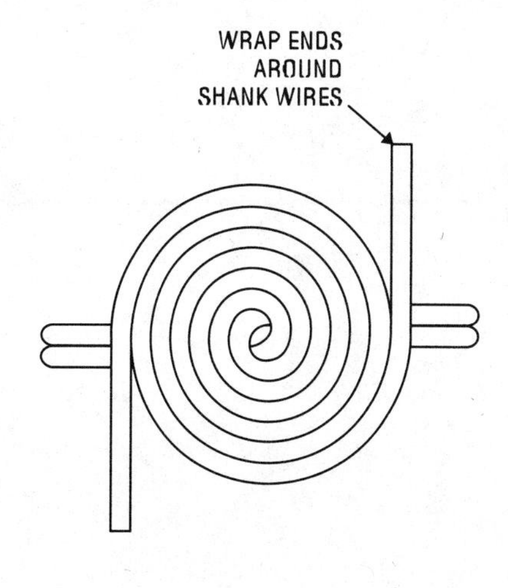

Diagram 6

#3 DOUBLE LOOP LOVE KNOT RING

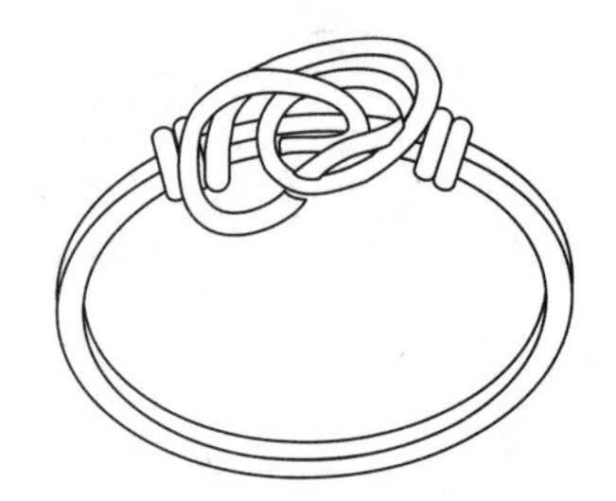

Double Loop Love Knot Ring

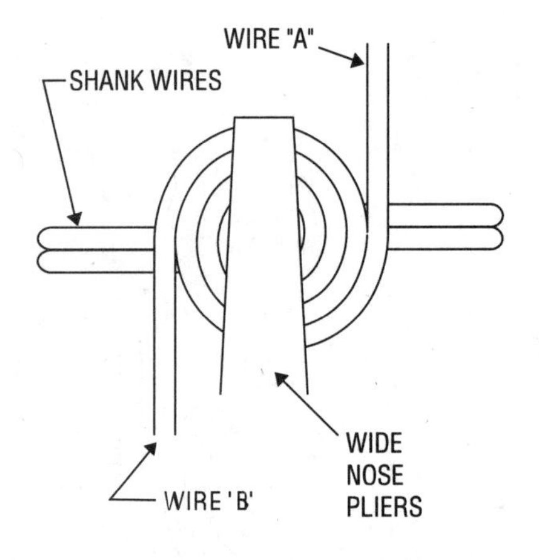

Diagram 7

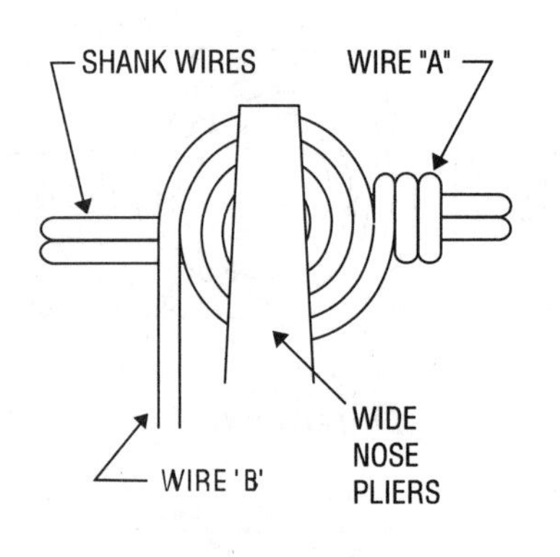

Diagram 8

For the best effect, use only 20 gauge round wire.

A. Follow directions for swirl ring. Be sure wires are swirled around each other **EXACTLY TWO** times. Also be sure to make the swirl very tight and as flat as possible from the very beginning of the swirl.

B. Hold finished swirl in jaws of wide nose pliers so ends of swirl wires are parallel (in opposite directions) to pliers as shown in *Diagram 7*.

C. Using chain nose pliers and while still holding swirl firmly with wide nose pliers, wrap wire A tightly around shank wires and cut off.

CAUTION: MAKE SURE SHANK WIRES DO NOT CROSS WHEN WRAPPING WIRE AROUND THEM.

D. Remove ring from pliers and turn it around so wire B is now where wire A was. Hold firmly in pliers again and repeat Step C above with wire B. *Diagrams 9 & 10*

E. Put ring back on mandrel as far as it will go. Using wide nose pliers, squeeze very firmly and evenly (where indicated in *Diagram 11*) and the swirl will pop into two interlocking loops. Ring is now complete and should look similar to *Double Loop Love Knot Ring* illustration on page 22.

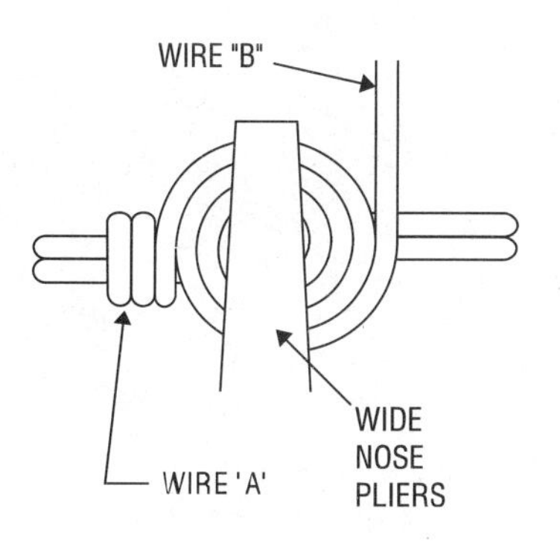

Diagram 9

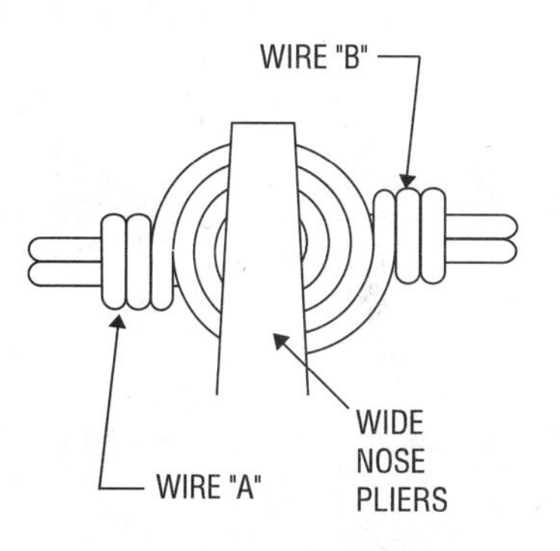

Diagram 10

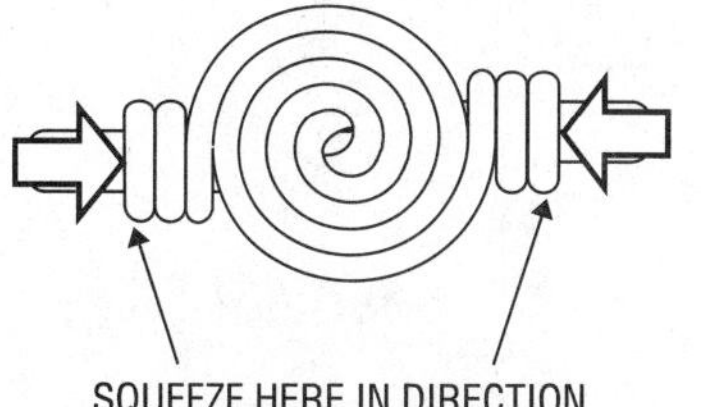

Diagram 11

#4 FANCY SWIRL LOOP RING

Fancy Loop Ring

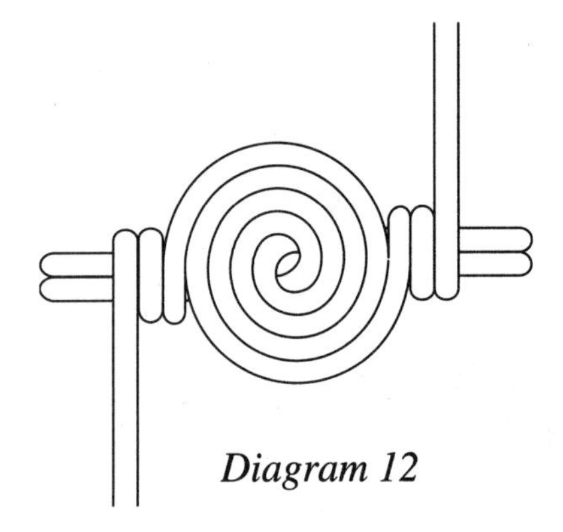

Diagram 12

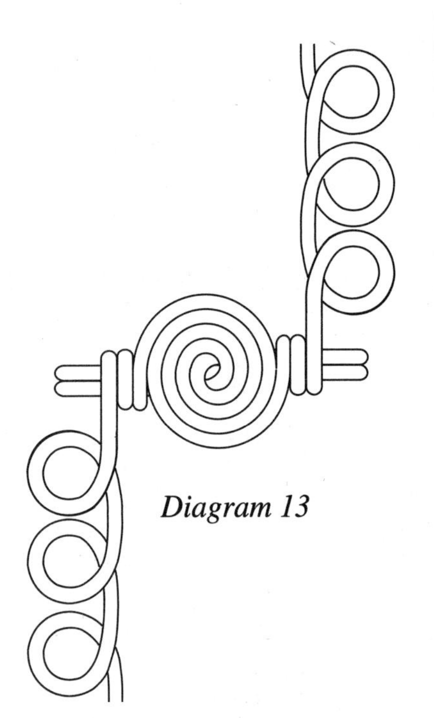

Diagram 13

A. Cut piece of 21 gauge round wire 12" long.

B. Repeat directions for Swirl Ring, except **DO NOT CUT OFF ENDS OF SWIRL WIRES**.

C. When swirl is complete, make sure wires are parallel to each other in opposite directions, perpendicular to shank wires. Wrap each around shank wires twice. *Diagram 12*

D. After swirl is anchored one per side, use needle nose pliers to make loops with remaining wires. (Three large loops or five small ones.) An odd number of loops is more appealing to the eye. *Diagram 13*

E. Do likewise with remaining wire. **BE SURE THE LOOPS ARE SAME SIZE AND EVENLY SPACED.**

F. Tie down each wire on opposite side of swirl. Cut off excess wire.

G. Put ring on mandrel and tap gently into shape.

#5 SCRAMBLED WIRE RING

A. Cut piece of round 21 gauge wire 10" long. Follow directions (A and B) for Swirl Ring except make only one and a half swirls with each wire and not as tight as Swirl Ring. Leave small space in swirl so you can tie down each side and still have room to push wire through openings, using the chain nose pliers.

B. Push (or pull) left wire through any small openings on right side. **DO NOT TIGHTEN**. Do same with right wire. Alternate procedure until most of wire is used.

C. Tie down ends as you would other wire rings.

D. Put ring on mandrel and flatten the jumble of wire with plastic hammer. If wire spreads too much, then tighten up the process as it is being done. The ring looks like a mess until this flattening stage. It is important to remember to pile wire high in early stages. Do not spread it out too much.

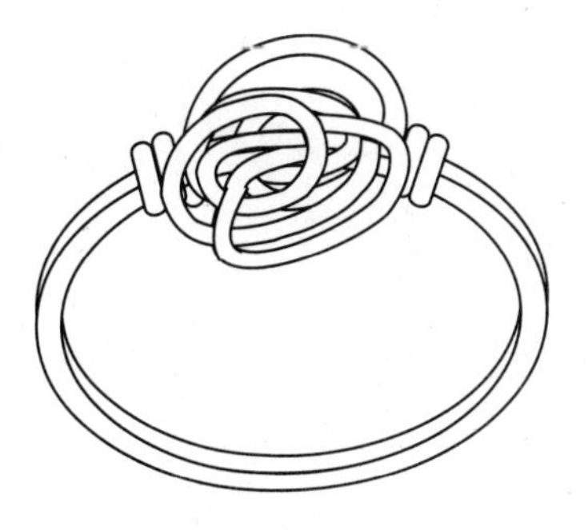

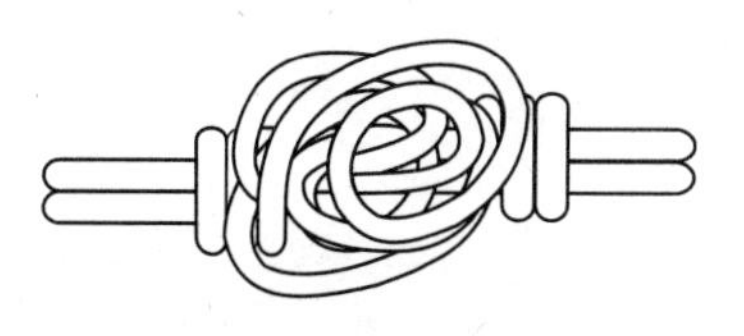

Scrambled Wire Ring

#6 PLAIN BEAD RING

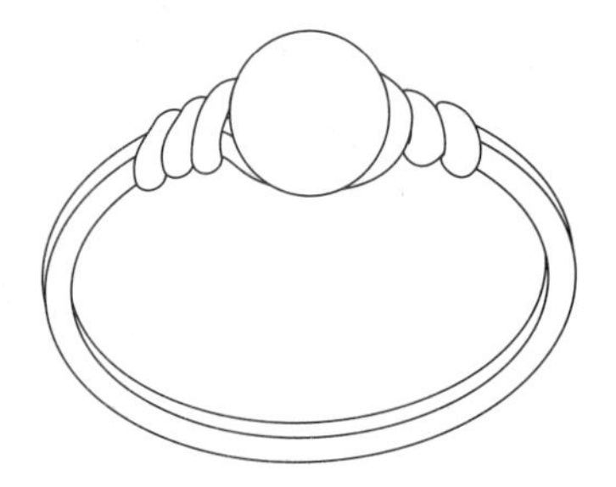

Plain Bead Ring

A. Cut one piece of round 21 gauge wire 8" long.

B. In center of wire, bend 90 degrees as shown. *Diagram 14*

C. Put 6mm bead on upright section of wire.

D. Bend upright wire parallel to horizontal wire. *Diagram 15*

E. Using wire nose pliers, bend wire as shown in *Diagram 16*. This will keep bead from slipping off wire as ring is being made.

F. Using grooved mandrel, put bead (with wire through it) in groove so wires are pointing down. Press bead down firmly with right hand thumb. Also make sure that as the wire is bent around mandrel, it is on desired (intended) size.

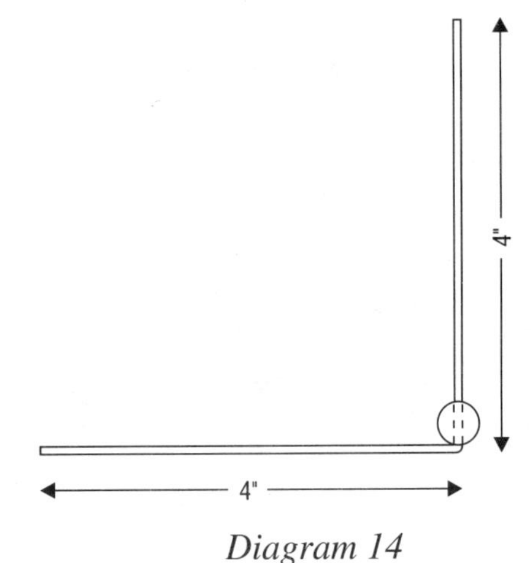

Diagram 14

Diagram 15

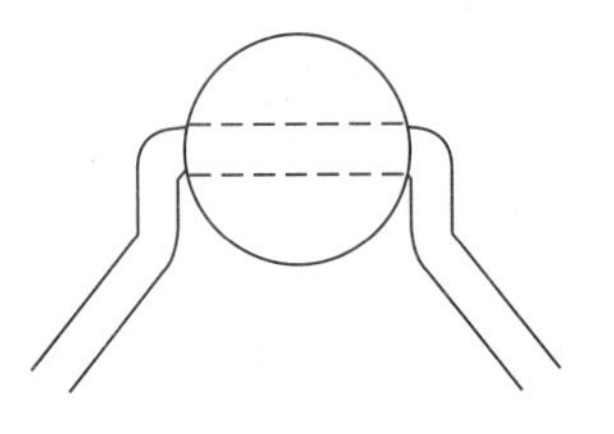

Diagram 16

G. Wrap wires around mandrel tightly in opposite directions making sure not to cross them. Bend wires across top of mandrel on opposite sides on bead. *Diagram 17*

H. Continue to bend wires snugly around bead, perpendicular across shank wires so each wrap wire is parallel to each other on opposite sides of bead. *Diagram 18*

I. Remove ring from mandrel and hold one side with wide nose pliers *(Diagram 19)* and wrap wire, on the same side, around shank wires next to bead. Two or three wraps are sufficient.

J. Do same to opposite side. Cut wire off at angle close to the shank.

K. Put ring on mandrel, shape and check size.

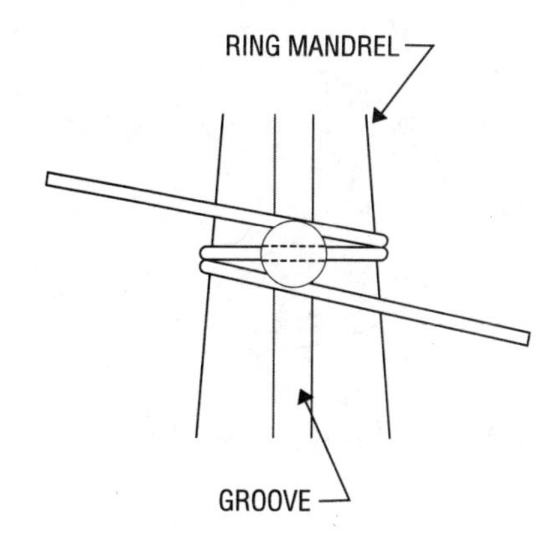

Diagram 17

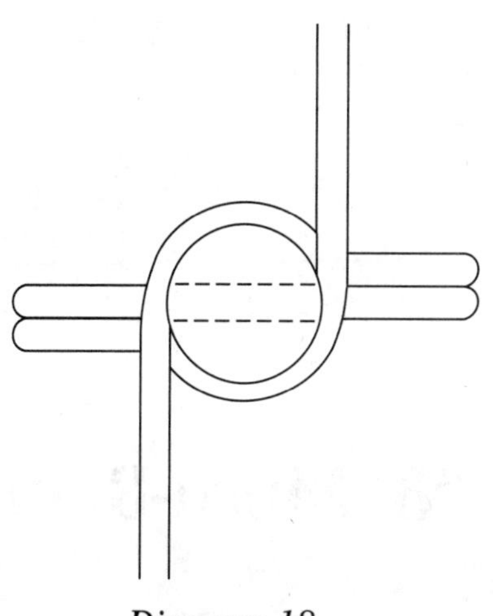

Diagram 18

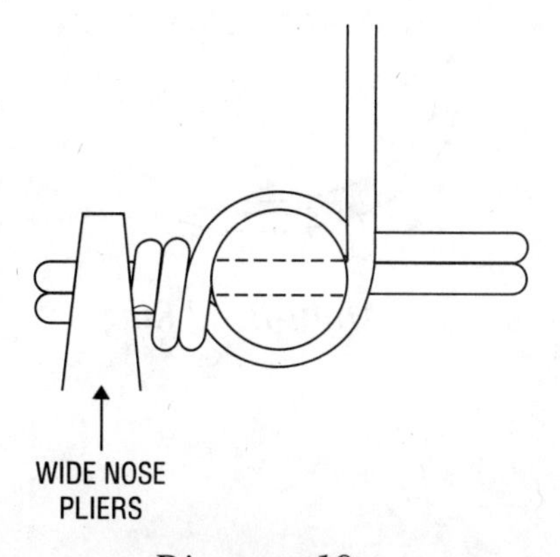

Diagram 19

#7 FANCY BEAD RING

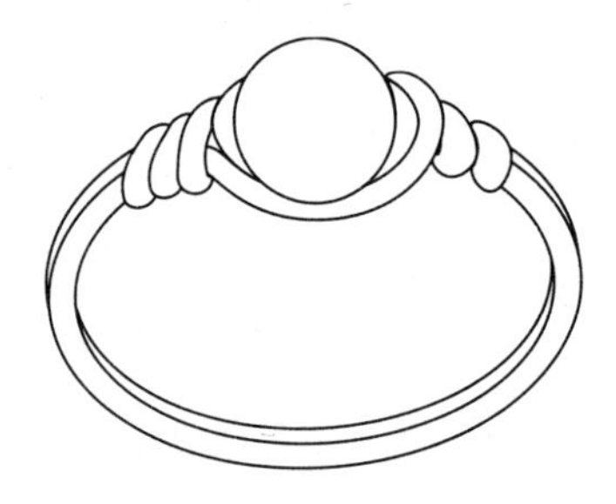

Fancy Bead Ring

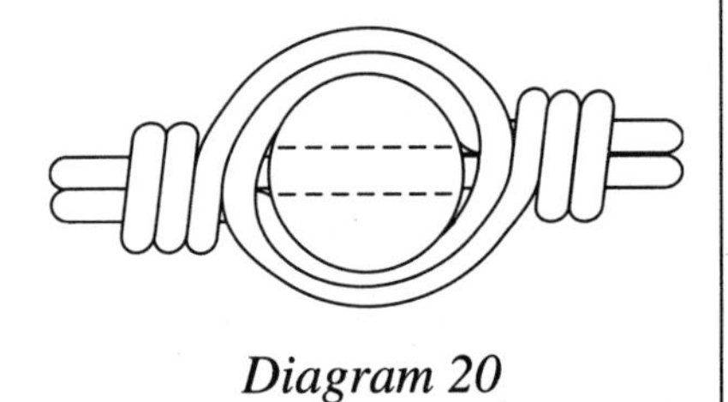

Diagram 20

A. Follow directions for Bead Ring (Steps A through K) with following exceptions:

1. Wire should be 10" - 12" long (round)

2. Do not cut off excess wire yet. Instead, wrap it parallel to bead on each side, both or one at a time. There is not a limit as to how many times you can wrap it around bead. (*Diagram 20*)

B. Tie down as usual, cut off at angle.

#8 MULTI-BEAD RING

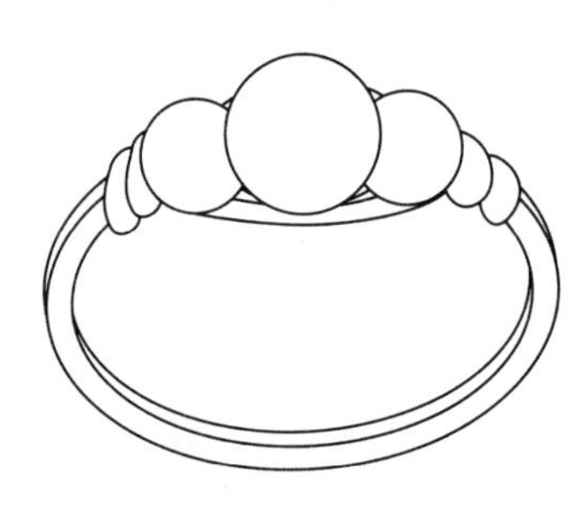

Multi-Bead Ring

A. Follow directions for Bead Ring except use piece of wire 10" long.

B. Triple Bead Ring is very popular. It can be made like a single bead ring using one 6mm and two 4mm beads as shown.

#9 MODIFIED BEAD RING

Large center bead (6mm) surrounded by six 4mm beads.

A. Follow Steps A through I for Plain Bead Ring *(pages 26-27)*. Wrap wires should be wrapped around shank wires one time. Do not cut off excess wrap wires.

B. Put three beads (4mm) on each wrap wire and tie down each wire on opposite side from where it originated.

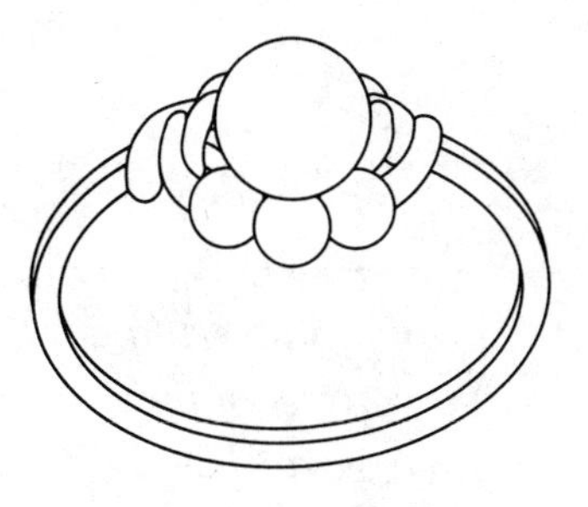

Modified Bead Ring

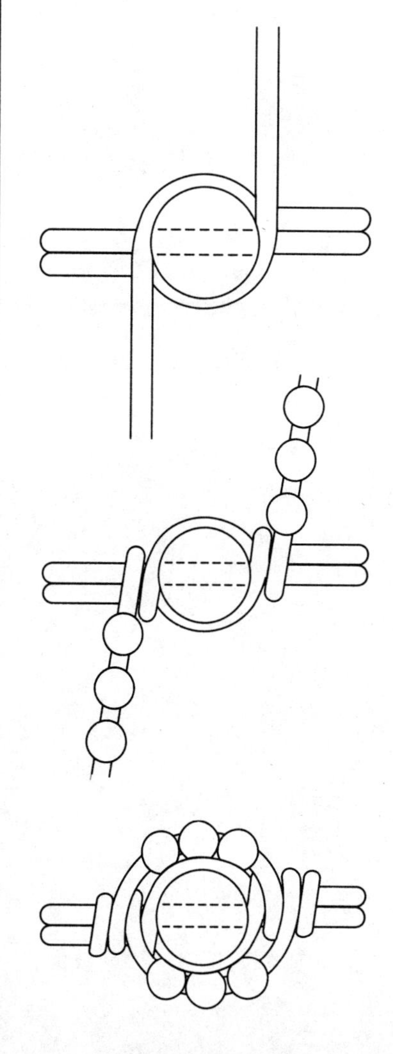

Diagram 21

#10 SIMPLE FREE FORM RING

See photo insert for variations of the Free Form Ring.

Of all wire wrap rings, the Free Form Ring is, without a doubt, a classic example of the unlimited possibilities. Stones of all shapes and sizes, cut, uncut, or faceted may be used. My favorite stone for a Free Form Ring is a large marquise cut. However, oval, oblong, square, baroque stones, or even undrilled beads look very nice when wirewrapped.

The wrap, in large part, is dictated by the shape, size, and color of the stone. "Let the stone do the talking." For example, I could not decide whether to wrap a crazy lace agate cabochon in gold or silver, so I combined twisted gold and silver to wrap a large 18mm x 25mm oval cut man's ring - five wires in all. The mixture of gold and silver enhanced the stone much more than if a single color had been used. The ring looked absolutely stunning because the stone demanded the mixture of gold and silver.

In this part of the chapter there are step by step diagrams of how to make a Simple Free Form Ring. The diagrams show a large marquise stone. **PLEASE REMEMBER, ANY SHAPE OR SIZE OF STONE MAY BE USED. THIS SYSTEM OF WRAPPING IS COMMON TO ALL FREE FORM RINGS OF THIS STYLE.**

In the directions, I have not suggested twisted wire, even though it may be used. For a three-wire Free Form, the center wire may be twisted, or, the two outside wires may be twisted and the center left plain. It is all a matter of personal choice.

The directions that follow are for a four-wire, all plain, Free Form. Top and bottom views are shown. If the written instructions seem vague, look at the drawings to see in detail where each wire is placed. The drawings are accurate.

The length of the pieces of wire used is determined by the size of the stone. The normal length for a 10mm x 14mm is 9". For a large stone 12mm x 30mm, use 10" lengths of wire. For extremely small stones, use two wires, average size stones use three wires, and extremely large stones use four.

WITH LARGE MARQUISE CUT STONE:

A. Cut four wires, 9" long (square wire, 20 or 21 gauge). Cut two wires, 4-1/2" long (square wire 20 or 21 gauge). Bend over the ends of these 4-1/2" wires 1/4". These will be the wrap wires.

B. Select a stone.

C. Put three *(or four as in Diagram 22)* 9" wires side by side, making sure they are even at ends. Wrap a short piece of tape around them, making sure tape is equal distance from each end of wires. Mark center.

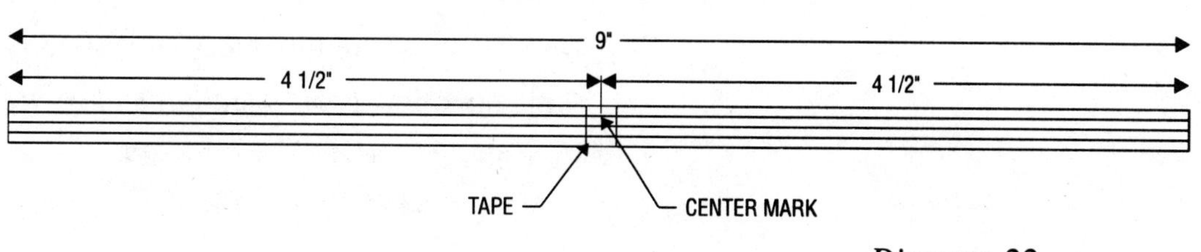

Diagram 22

D. With felt tip pen, mark the place for each wrap wire:

1. For a size 6 ring, measure 3/4" from each side of center mark. This is where each of wrap wires will begin.

2. For every two sizes larger, increase distance of each wrap wire form center by 1/16".

3. For sizes four and five, decrease this distance by 1/16".

4. Wrap wires toward outer edges of group wires.

E. For a size six ring, total inside distance between wraps should be 1-1/2". *Diagram 23*

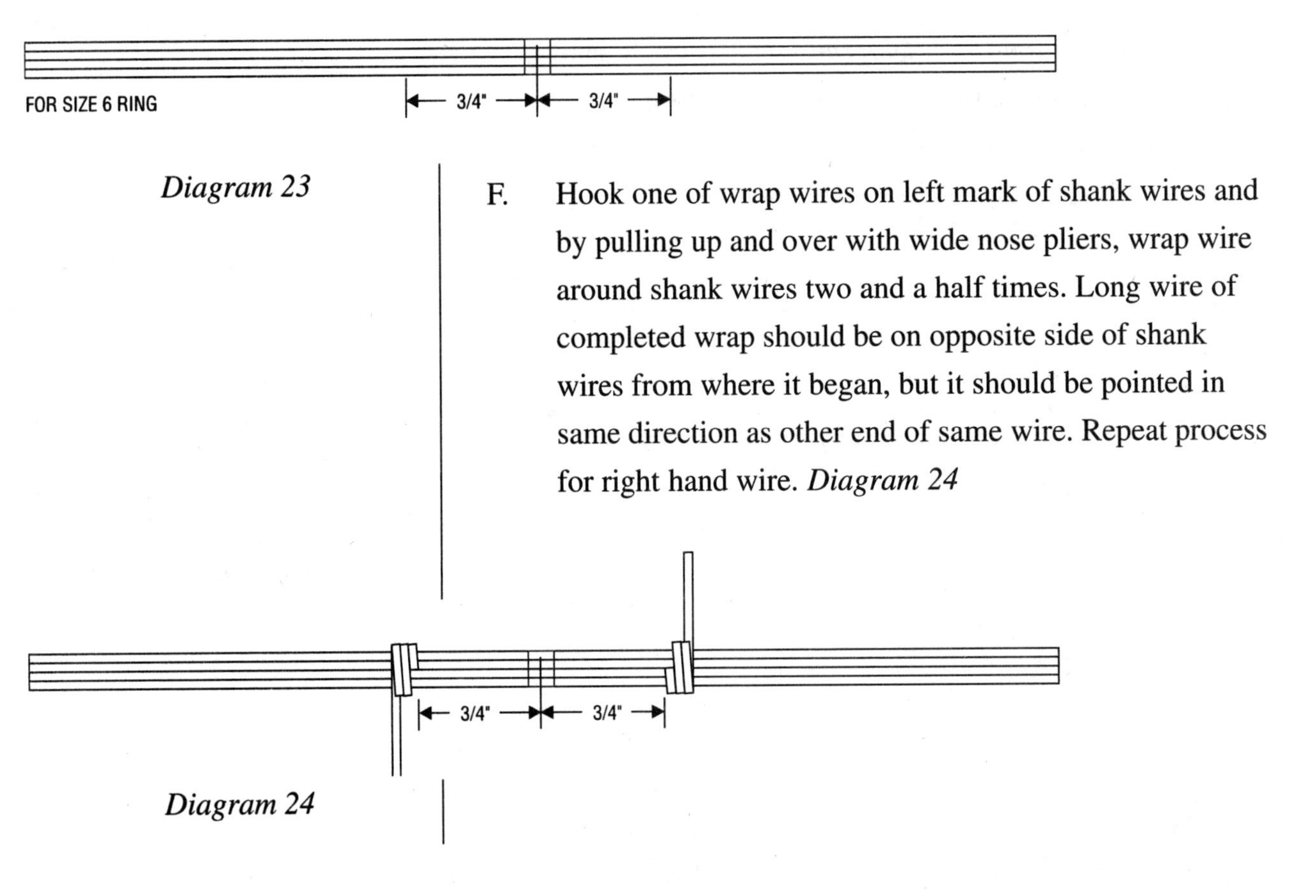

Diagram 23

F. Hook one of wrap wires on left mark of shank wires and by pulling up and over with wide nose pliers, wrap wire around shank wires two and a half times. Long wire of completed wrap should be on opposite side of shank wires from where it began, but it should be pointed in same direction as other end of same wire. Repeat process for right hand wire. *Diagram 24*

Diagram 24

G. Remove tape from shank wires.

H. Bend shank wires around ring mandrel one size smaller than intended size. Before this is done, make sure that ring mandrel is in space between wrap wires, and the long end of wrap wires is on **OUTSIDE** of shank wires. Check *Diagram 25* for direction confirmation.

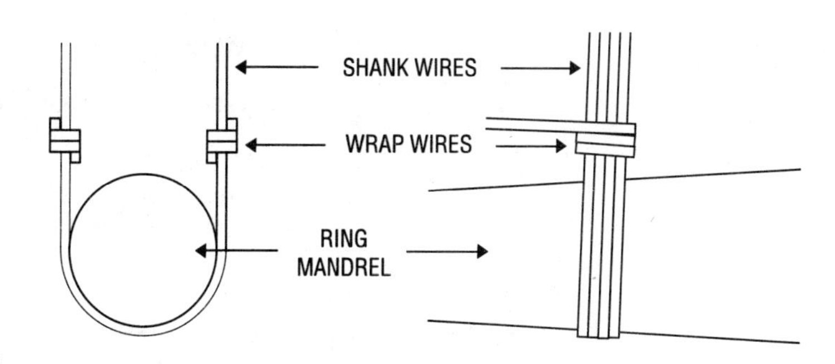

Diagram 25

I. Continue bending shank wires around top of mandrel as shown in *Diagram 26.*

Diagram 26

J. Make U turn with shank wires closest to you. This is done while shank wires are still on mandrel. Press down hard and firm with right thumb while grasping wires firmly and making circular motion. Forefinger and thumb of right hand will be holding shank wires tight up against mandrel. *Diagram 27*

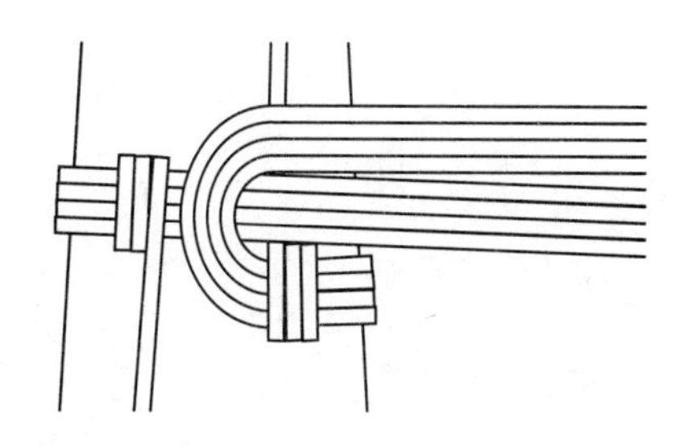

Diagram 27

(ALL DRAWINGS ENLARGED FOR CLARITY.)

K. Do likewise with second set of shank wires. *Diagram 28*

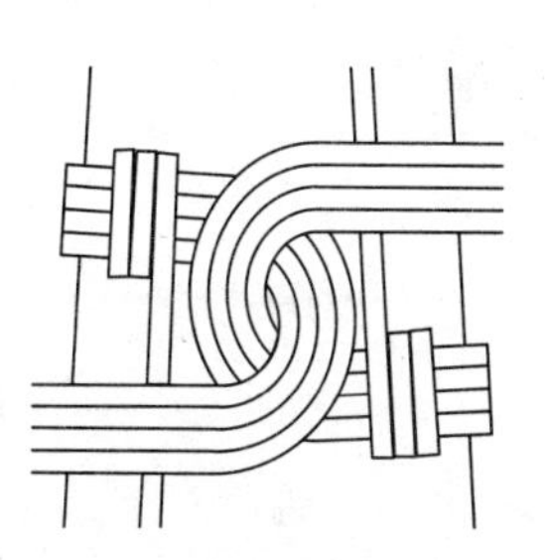

Diagram 28

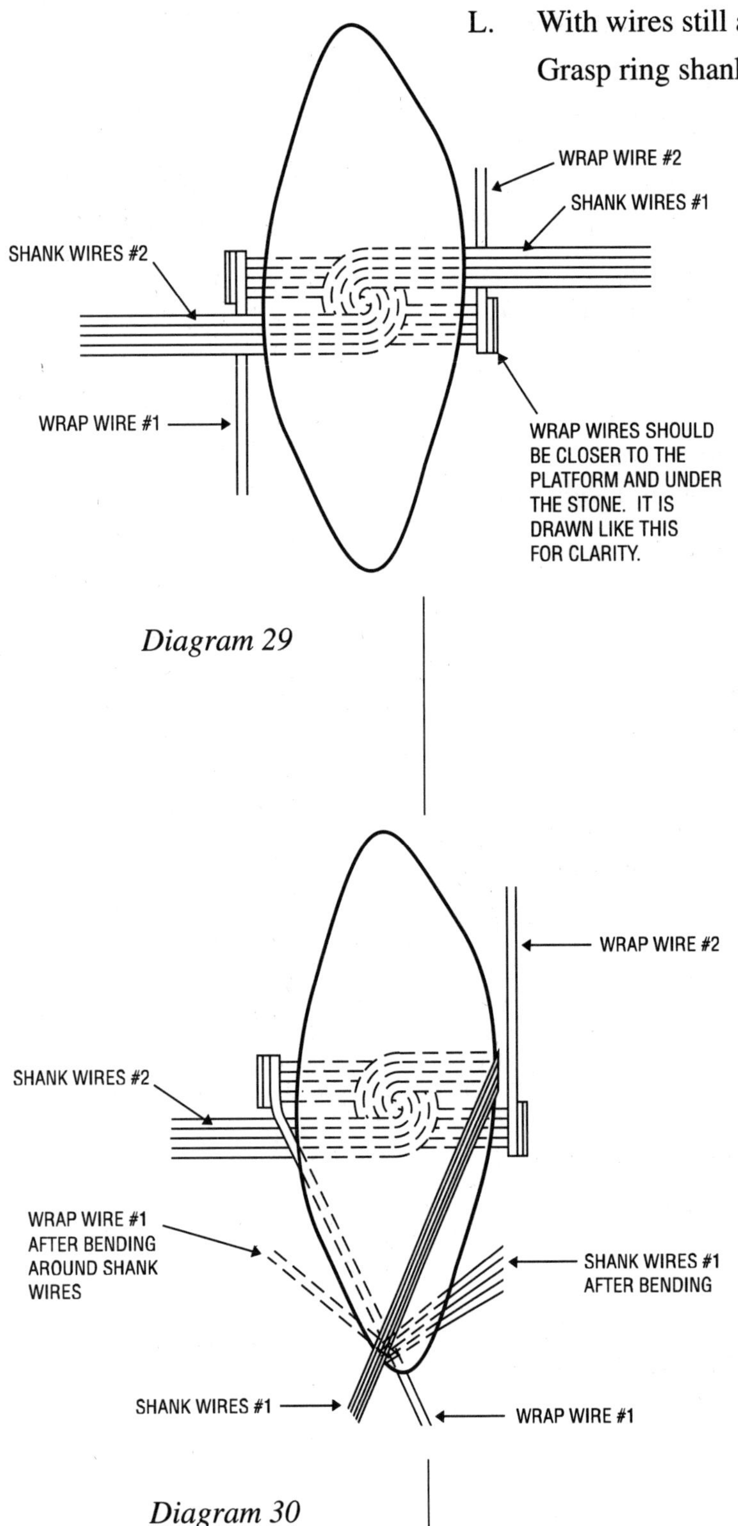

Diagram 29

Diagram 30

L. With wires still around mandrel, lay mandrel in left hand. Grasp ring shank on either side of thumb and forefinger. Pull ring shank toward you and tap gently on top of ring shank (where wires cross each other) with plastic hammer until it (the ring) slips down to intended size. Where wires cross shall now be referred to as **PLATFORM**. Remove ring mandrel.

M. Place flat side of stone on platform so platform is directly in center of stone. *Diagram 29*

N. With left hand, hold stone (on platform) between thumb and forefinger, thumb on top, **PRESSING HARD!! IT IS ABSOLUTELY IMPERATIVE STONE DOES NOT SLIP AS YOU BEGIN WRAPPING IT**. Grasp shank wires 1 in your right hand and bend them all up and at same time, bend them along right edge of stone. When shank wires 1 reaches other end of stone; make sure wrap wires 1 are sandwiched between shank wires 1 and under side of stone; then bend group wires down and underneath stone back in opposite direction. *Diagram 30*

O. Bend wrap wire 1 back (180 degrees) in opposite direction (to left) so it is parallel to left side of stone as seen from top. It should be keeping shank wires from slipping off edge of stone. *Diagram 31*

P. Do likewise with shank wires 2 and wrap wires 2 and repeat Step O for wrap wire also. Ring should now look like *Diagram 32.*

Top view of how ring should look at this point.

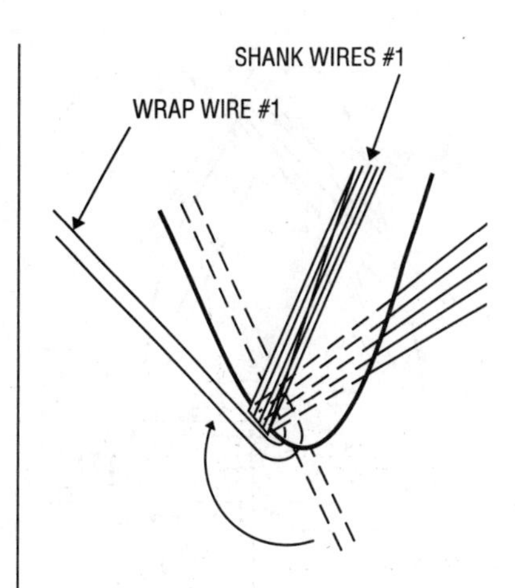

Diagram 31

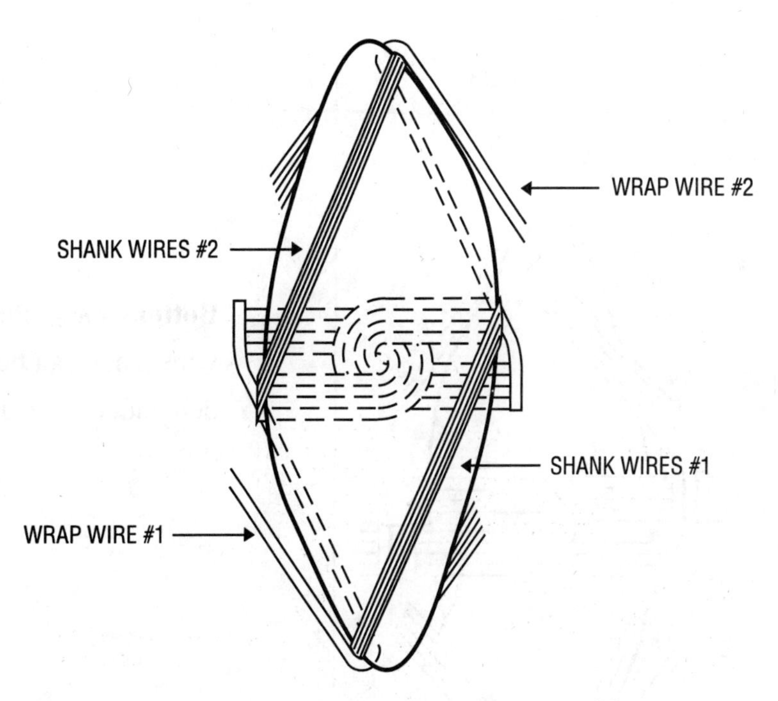

Diagram 32

From this point on, only BOTTOM VIEWS will be shown until final steps.

Follow visual diagrams as close as possible.

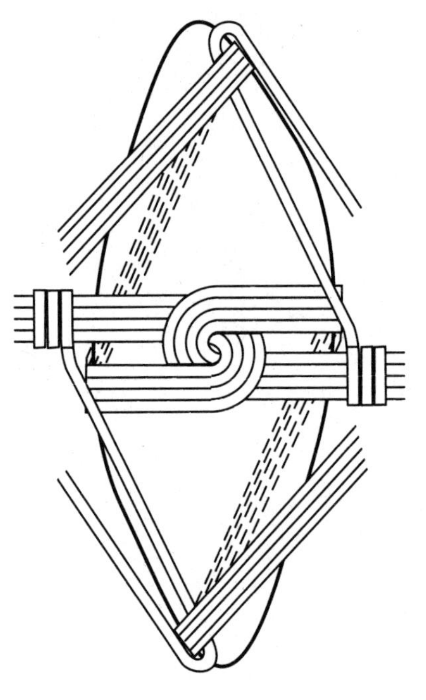

Diagram 33

Only BOTTOM VIEWS will be shown until final steps.

The wrap wires around shank can be closer to platform and under stone so they are hidden from view. *Diagram 32* shows them out farther on shank to facilitate clarity.

Bottom view of large marquise Free Form using four wires is shown in *Diagram 33*. Section of shank wires going around finger has been omitted in order to show placement of other wires.

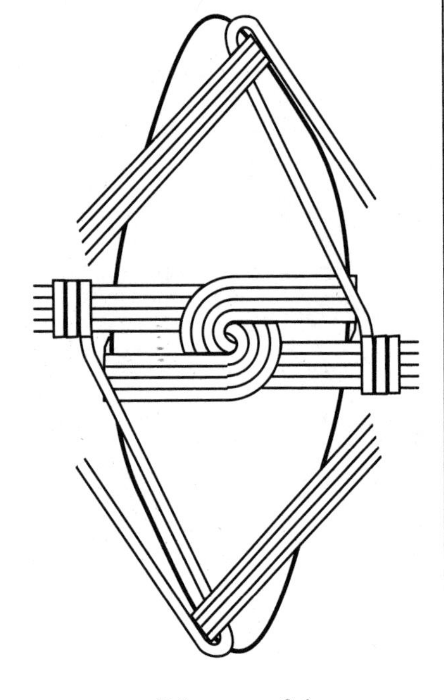

Diagram 34

Bottom View: Please note once again position of wrap wire. They can be closer to platform so they will be hidden under stone and not seen from top. *Diagram 34*

Q. Hold with wide nose pliers (see large arrows) and bend wrap wire back 1/4" as indicated. *Diagram 35*

This process makes wrap wires more snug around shank wires as well as giving added dimension to wrap.

R. Note wrap wires in *Diagram 36.*

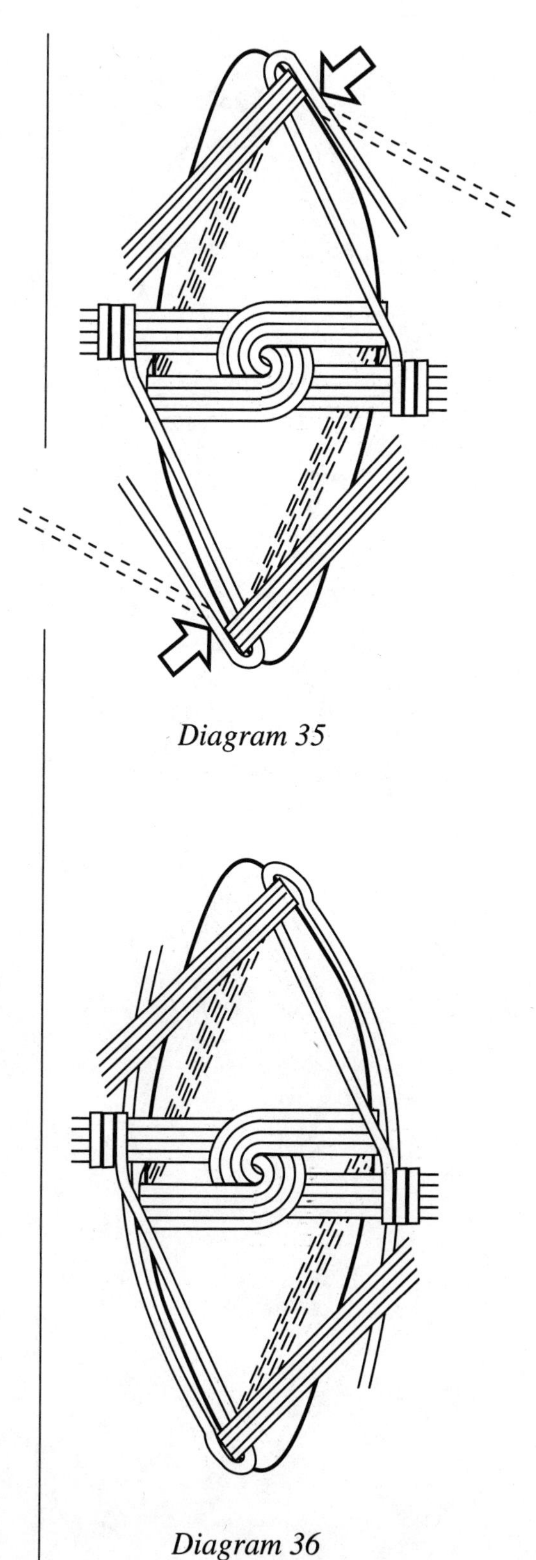

Diagram 35

Diagram 36

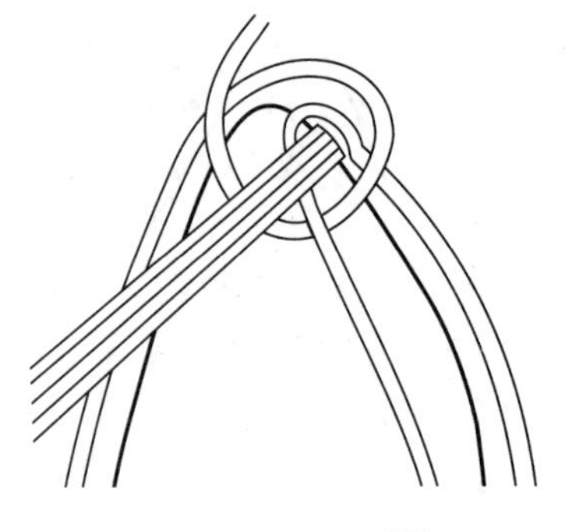

Diagram 37

S. **Bottom View** (*Diagram 37*): Enlarged diagram of wrap wire tie in. Should be wrapped twice around and much tighter than shown. After second time around, cut off wire so the end is under the shank wires. Repeat this process for other wrap wires.

T. **Top View** (*Diagram 38)*: Bend both sets of shank wires up vertically, make sure they are outside of wrap wires. Cut off shank wires so they are long enough to wrap over wrap wires as shown.

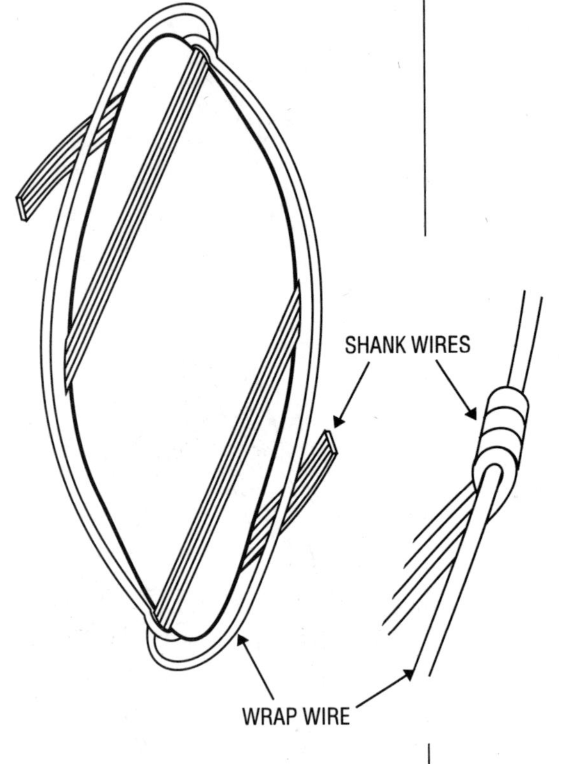

Diagram 38

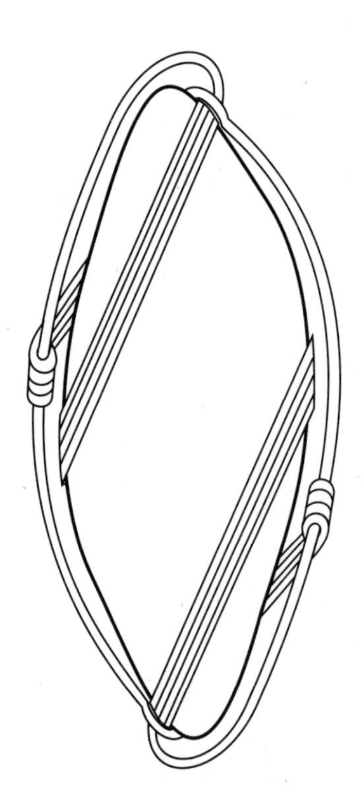

Diagram 39: Finished Free Form Marquise

#11 FANCY FREE FORM RING

The Fancy Free Form Ring is any variation of the regular Free Form Ring with added swirls or loops from longer wire. This ring is very similar in technique except for a few minor changes. Use three or four wires and select any shape stone. It would be best if the stone is no shorter than 14mm.

See photo insert for the Fancy Free Form Ring.

A. Follow steps outlined for Simple Free Forms (four wire) Ring A through N - **EXCEPT DO NOT** bend all of four shank wires over across the top of stone . **INSTEAD**, bend over one wire, make sure it is inside wire (one closest to center of group wires). **TREAT THAT ONE WIRE AS THOUGH IT WAS ALL OF THE GROUP WIRES.** If this is not done it will not be possible to successfully complete this ring. **ABOVE ALL, HAVE PATIENCE**, it can be done and the end result is really worth it.

B. If you have completed instructions to this point, ring should resemble this diagram:

DO NOT CUT OFF ANY WIRES WHATSOEVER (YET)

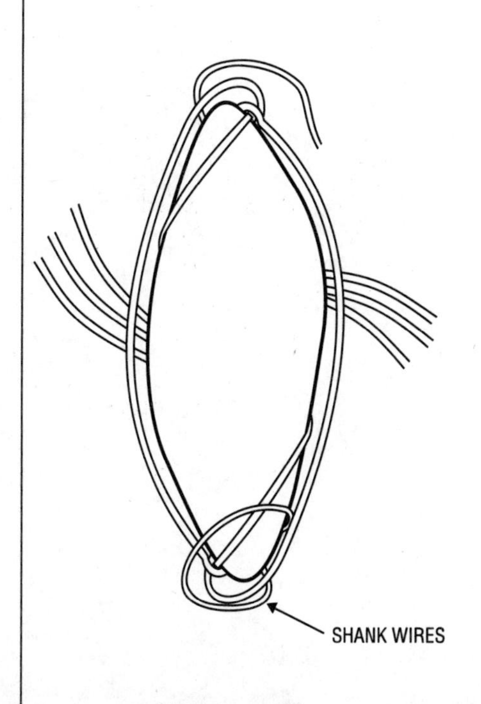

Diagram 40

C. With excess wrap wire, make loop on top (end) of stone in opposite direction and tie down underneath. Do likewise with other wrap wires. Try to make loop small and flowing.

D. Alternating with each end, take each of group wires, one at a time, loop it through loop already made and tie down underneath at opposite end of stone. Confusing? Let yourself go and ad-lib with each remaining wire. Be sure to run it through previously made loop and follow the general contour of stone. Do not cover top of stone, only the sides. Tie down underneath out of the way. Practice a lot with brass, it's fun!!!

E. If directions at this stage seem inadequate, perhaps they are, but how else can one learn except by doing and doing... and doing... and doing.

#12 FREE FORM SHARK'S TOOTH RING

See photo insert for the Free Form Shark's Tooth Ring.

A. Use same directions for baroque (or marque) stone Free Form Ring except for the following modifications:

1. Use four wires instead of three.

2. Wrap should be as indicated in *Diagram 41*:

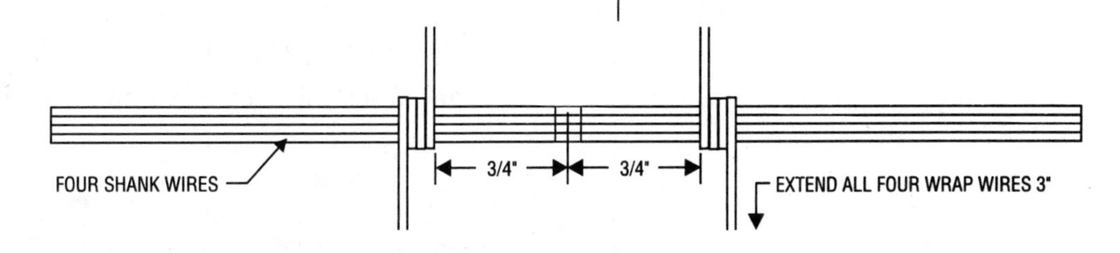

Diagram 41

B. Use only a curved tooth.

C. Divide set of group wires on **RIGHT** into two groups of wires each. (This will be after platform is made.) Two of the wires will be wrapped around point of tooth and other two as indicted. *Diagram 42*

D. This requires a lot of experimentation and total familiarity with the free form system as previously described.

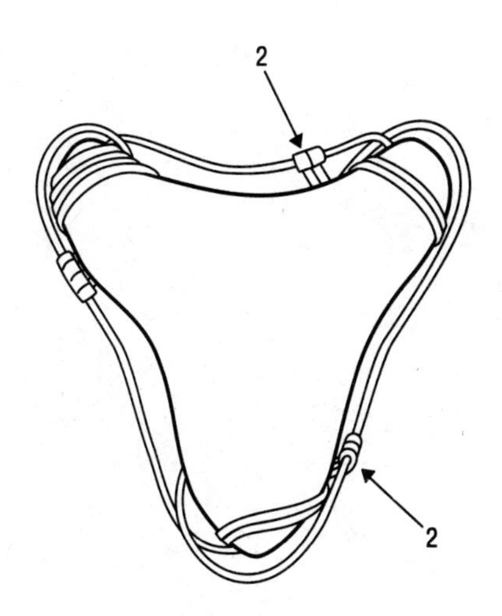

Diagram 42

#13 STANDARD FORM RING

See cover & photo insert for the Standard Form Ring.

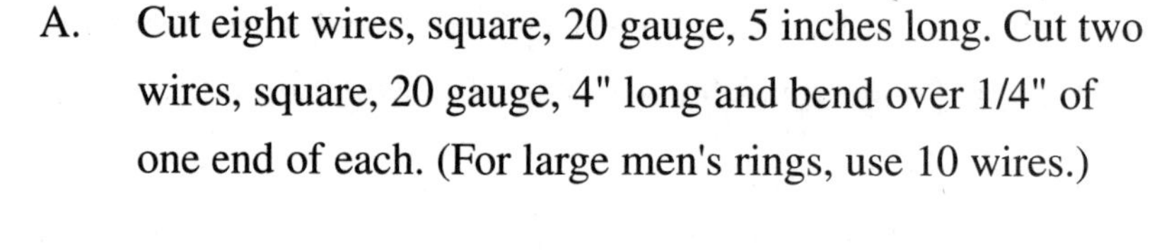

A. Cut eight wires, square, 20 gauge, 5 inches long. Cut two wires, square, 20 gauge, 4" long and bend over 1/4" of one end of each. (For large men's rings, use 10 wires.)

B. Tape eight wires together and mark on tape midway between end of wires.

C. Consult chart on page 47 for distance between center mark and wrap wire. Example: Size 5-1/2: 9/16" from center mark.

D. Make four complete wraps around eight group wires. Be sure wraps are tight and snug. Do likewise with other wrap wire and remove tape.

E. Bend wires around mandrel two sizes smaller than intended size. If you are making a size 5-1/2, bend group wires around that portion of mandrel which measures size 3-1/2. *Diagram 44*

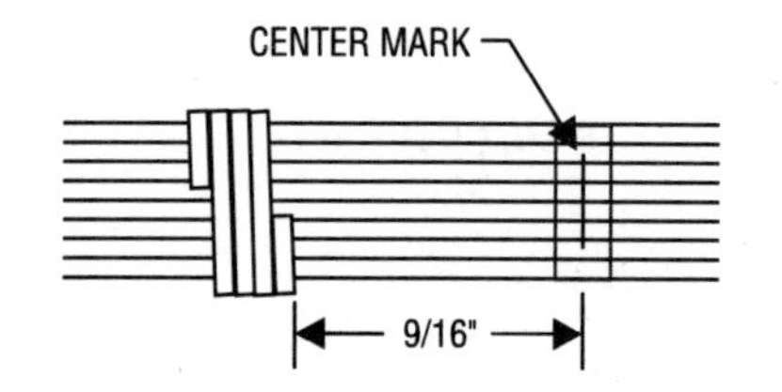

Diagram 43

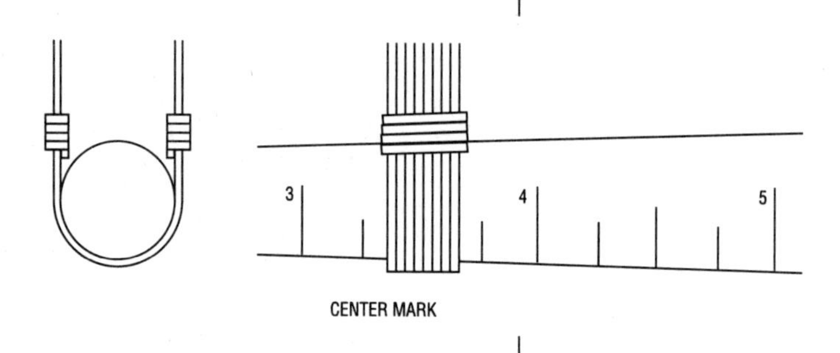

Diagram 44

F. Remove wires from mandrel and using wide blade pocket knife, bend up one outside wire on each side as shown in *Diagram 45*.

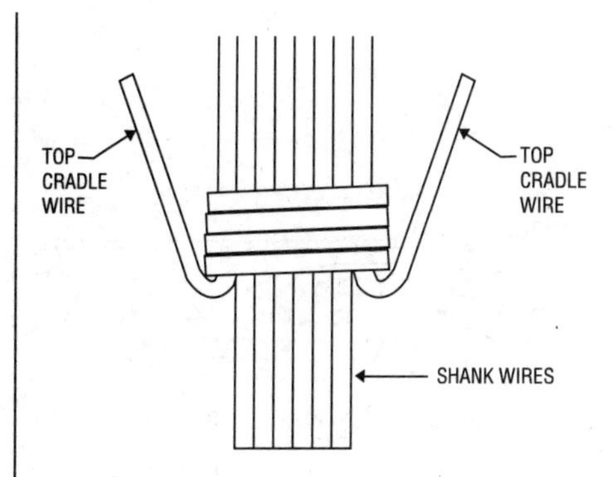

Diagram 45

G. Hold assembled wires by thumb and first two fingers of each hand. Cradle shank wires between first and second finger so the **WRAP** wires are parallel to the ground and place thumbs on top surface of wrap wires on either side. Press shank wires firmly on flat surface and at same time, with thumb nails. Slide wrap wires down about 1/16" (a shade more for an exceptionally high dome cabochon.) **DO NOT DO THIS FOR FLAT STONES.**

H. Now bend up two more shank wires as you did in Step F. *Diagram 46*

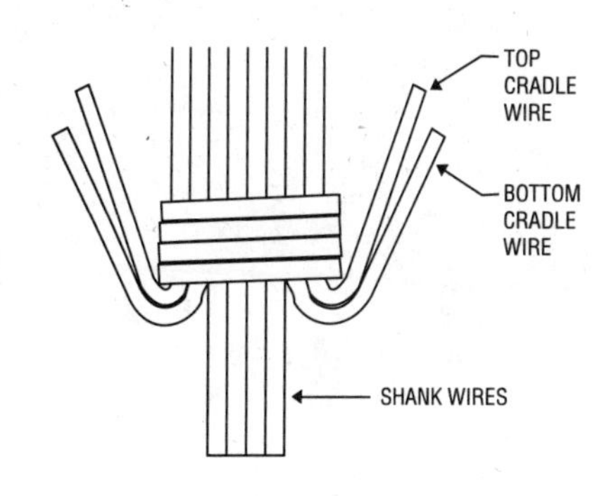

Diagram 46

I. Put assembly on ring mandrel and size properly before inserting cabochon.

J. Insert cabochon as shown. Important to **KEEP CRADLE WIRES AS CLOSE TO TIP END OF CABOCHON AS POSSIBLE.** *Diagram 47*

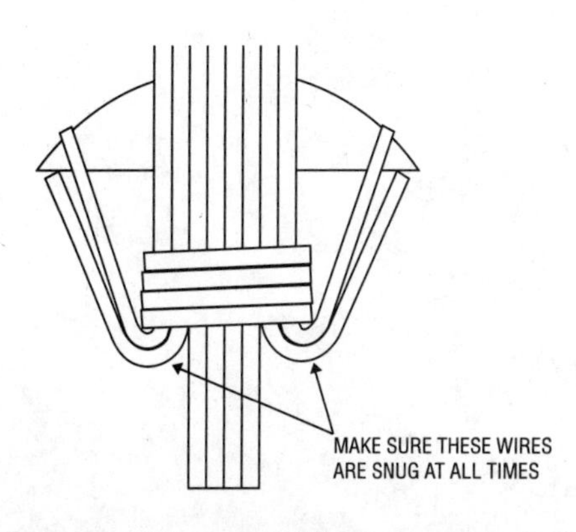

Diagram 47

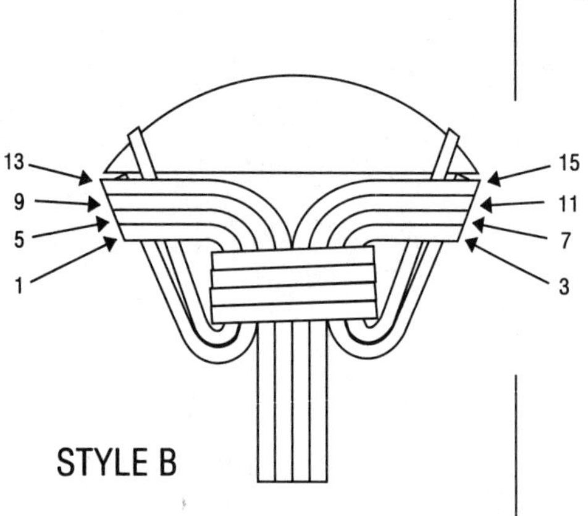

Diagram 48

K. The shank wires coming up past stone can now be separated and bent as shown, ONE AT A TIME, as in style A, B, or C. See page 46.
IT IS IMPORTANT TO BEND, CUT, AND TUCK ONE WIRE AT A TIME, ALTERNATING OPPOSITE SIDES AND CORNERS OF RING. *DIAGRAM 48* SHOWS ORDER OF CUTTING AND TUCKING WIRES. EVEN NUMBERS ARE ON OTHER SIDE OF RING.

L. After each set of four wires is bent, cut, and tucked, it is important to put rings on mandrel to make sure it is still on the intended size. Rings have a tendency to shrink as each set of four wires are bent, cut, and tucked. **IT IS ALSO IMPERATIVE TO MAKE SURE THE RING IS THE INTENDED SIZE BEFORE THE FOUR INSIDE WIRES ARE BENT, CUT, AND TUCKED. THE LAST FOUR INSIDE WIRES CONTROL SIZING OF RING.**

M. Any of the wires can be twisted at this time before the process of bending, cutting, and tucking.

N. After all shank wires are in place, lock wires will be added in order to make the stone more secure in the setting. The number of wires on each side will be determined by style and design you have chosen. (See styles A, B, or C on page 46.) Cut lock wires long enough to overlap so they can be tucked under and cut off. Add one wire at a time on alternating sides. Any number of lock wires can be added as long as they are functional; maximum of 3 per side. All lock wires should be twisted. *Diagram 49*

Personally, I consider anything over three lock wires excessive. Also, Style C requires no lock wires at all. The tucked in shank wires cover up each corner of stone.

O. Using chain nose pliers, place end of jaws of chain nose pliers at points X and Y. *(Diagram 50)* Pliers will be perpendicular to side of ring. Squeeze gently, but very firmly. Be careful not to let jaws of pliers slip and scratch wire. If this is done properly, you will get the effect shown in *Diagram 51*.

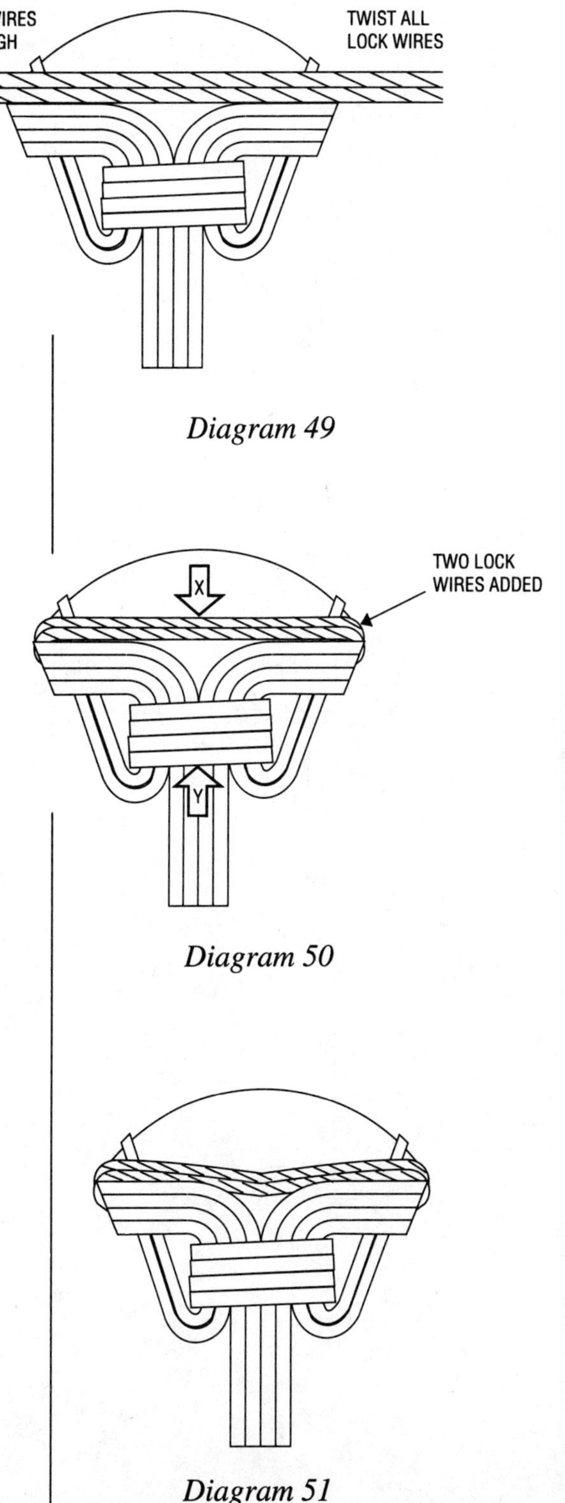

Diagram 49

Diagram 50

Diagram 51

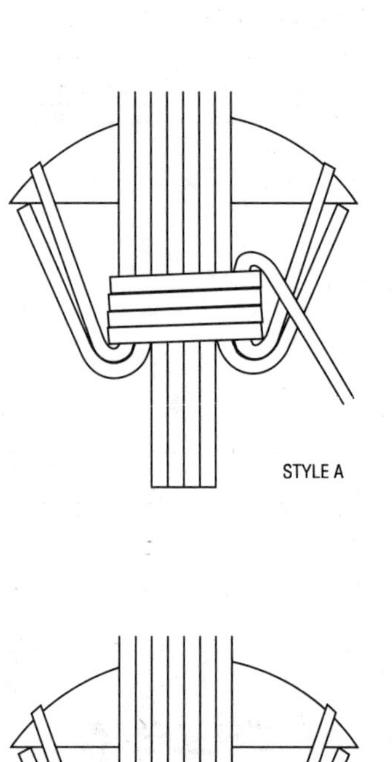

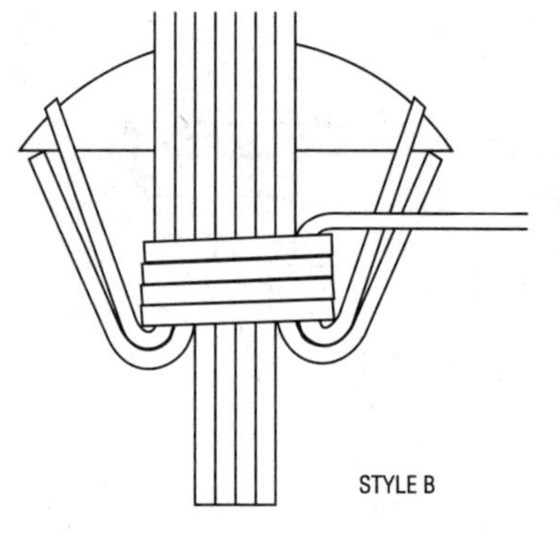

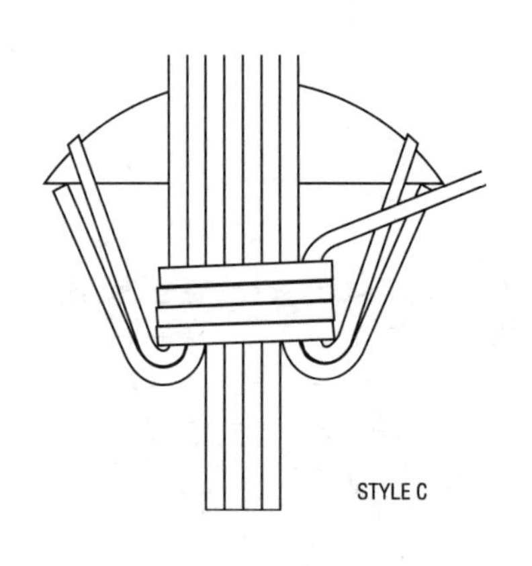

No additional **LOCK WIRES** required for Style C.

CHART FOR WRAPWIRES

RING SIZE	4 to 5-1/2	6 to 7-1/2	8 to 9-/12	10 to 11-1/2	12 to 13-1/2	14 to 14-1/2
Distance between wrap wire and center mark	1/2" to 9/16"	5/8"	11/16"	3/4" to 13/16"	13/16" to 7/8"	1"

DISTANCES BETWEEN WRAP WIRES ARE TO BE MEASURED ALWAYS FROM CENTER MARK.

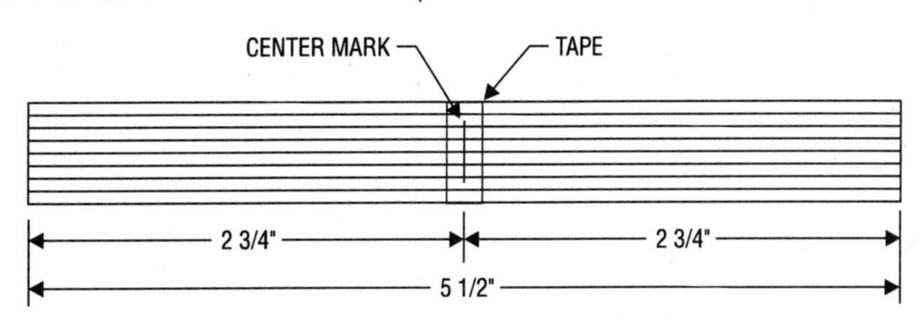

Diagram 52

1. This chart is very flexible. Different wrappers have different styles. This chart is a product of my successes and preferences. I prefer the stone in Standard Form Ring to set well above wrap wires (higher than most wrappers). The figures in this chart are arranged accordingly. This chart is for stones 12mm x 14mm.

2. For stones larger than 12mm x 14mm - 18mm x 25mm, add 1/16".

3. For stones 20mm x 25mm, add 1/8" - 3/16".

4. For high dome stones 18mm x 25mm, add 3/16".

5. For 22mm x 30mm standard form 12 wire bracelet, wrap wires should be 1-1/8" from center mark.

6. For 30mm x 40mm standard form 14 wire bracelet, wrap wires should be 1-5/16" from center mark.

#1 SIMPLE WIRE BRACELET: THREE WIRE BRAIDED

A. Cut one wire 18" long. Cut one wire 9-1/2" long and bend up one end 1/2". Cut two wires 3" long and bend up end of each one 1/4". **(ALL OF THESE WIRES ARE 22 GAUGE SQUARE.)**

B. Grip, at halfway point, the 18" wire with large part of the jaws of needle nose pliers and make once complete turn around it. *Diagram 53*

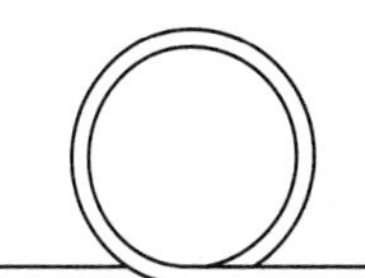
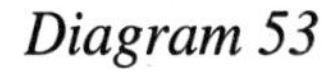

Diagram 53

C. At base of loop, use wide nose pliers to bend as shown in *Diagram 54.*

Diagram 54

D. Put 9-1/2" piece of wire in middle of two wires. Make sure the 1/2" bent up end is in loop just made. *Diagram 55.*

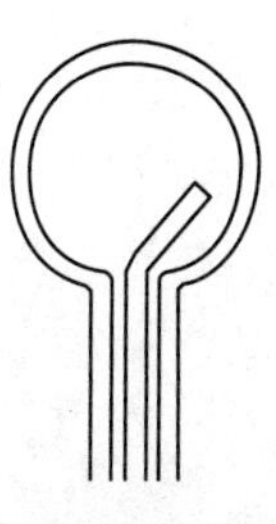

Diagram 55

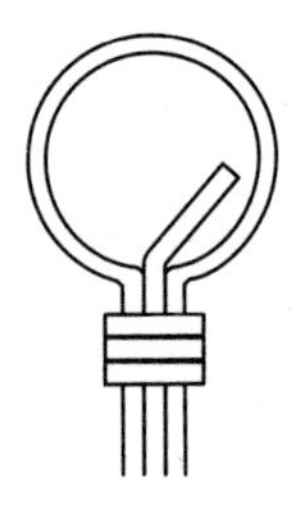

Diagram 56

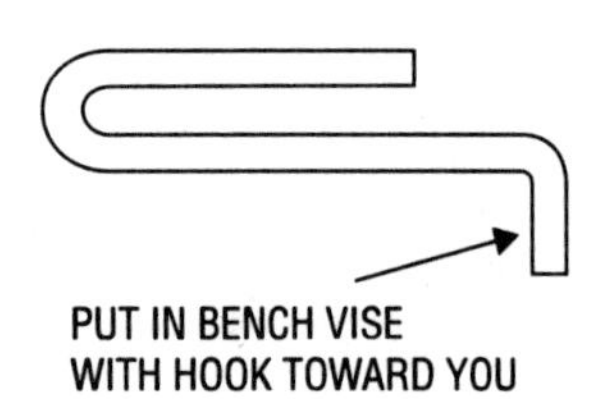

Diagram 57

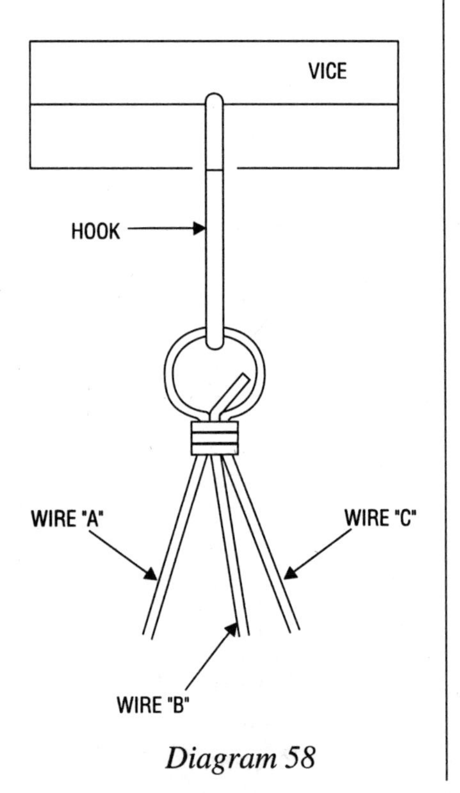

Diagram 58

E. Put on wrapwire as shown. *Diagram 56*

F. Using a 3" piece of scrap wire, bend as shown in *Diagram 57.*

G. Put looped end on hook and spread wires.

H. If you know how to make a pigtail, the rest is simple. Entire bracelet is braided until a length of 7" is reached. If you are not familiar with braiding then refer to *Diagram 58-62*. Each wire is lettered for what is to follow.

I. Take wire C and put it over wire B so it is parallel and next to wire A. *Diagram 59*

J. Now take wire A and put it over wire C so it is next to and parallel to wire B. *Diagram 60*

(FOR CLARITY, WIRES ARE SHOWN SPREAD OUT. IN REALITY THEY SHOULD BE CLOSE AT THE WRAP WIRE.)

K. Now take wire B and put it over wire A so it is next to and parallel with wire C. *Diagram 61*

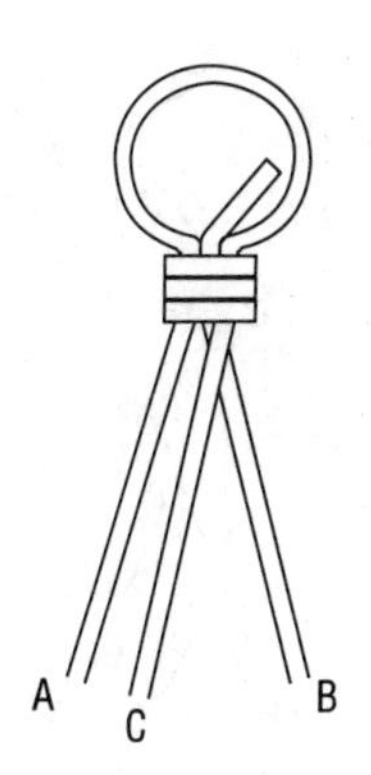

Diagram 59

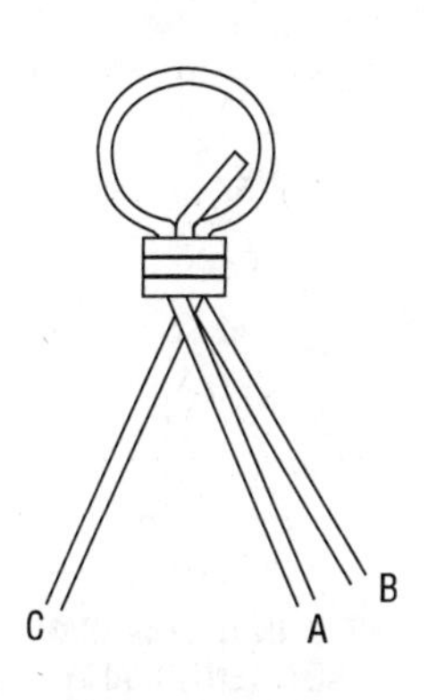

Diagram 60

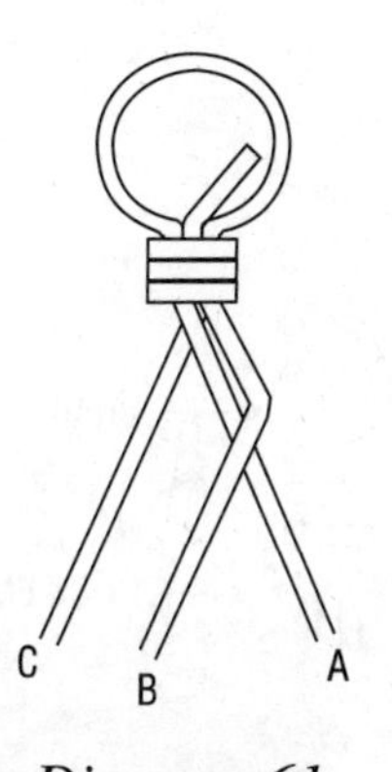

Diagram 61

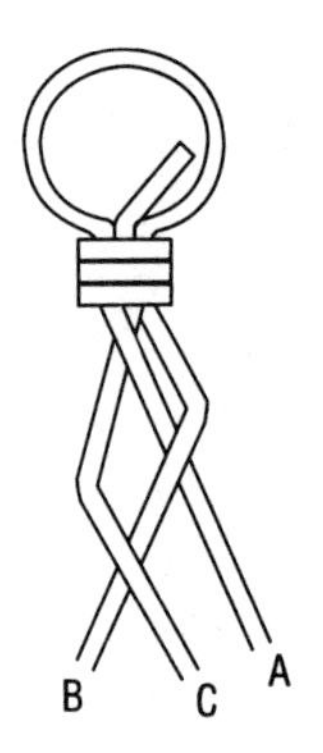

Diagram 62

L. Now take wire C and put it over wire B so it is next to and parallel with wire A. *Diagram 62*

M. The braided pattern is beginning to emerge. Repeat Steps I through L until you have a 7" braid. The pattern shown here is very, very loose so as to show wire position and clarify detail. In reality, **DO NOT MAKE BRAID THIS LOOSE; HOWEVER, DO NOT MAKE IT EXTREMELY TIGHT EITHER — REMEMBER WIRE JEWELRY SHOULD LOOK DELICATE.**

N. Always remember to maintain a good even braid pattern. Take highest outside wire and bend it over center one so it is parallel to wire on opposite side from where you started.

WIRES IN THE DIAGRAM ARE INTENTIONALLY SPREAD FOR CLARITY

Diagram 63

O. Remove bracelet from hook on vise. Cut off overhang from piece in center of loop.

P. Using closed vise as an anvil, take plastic hammer and **GENTLY** flatten bracelet from end to end.

Q. At this point, unfinished hook should look like Diagram 63. (Wires in the diagram are intentionally spread for clarity.) Bend the ends of braid so wires A, B, and C are parallel to each other.

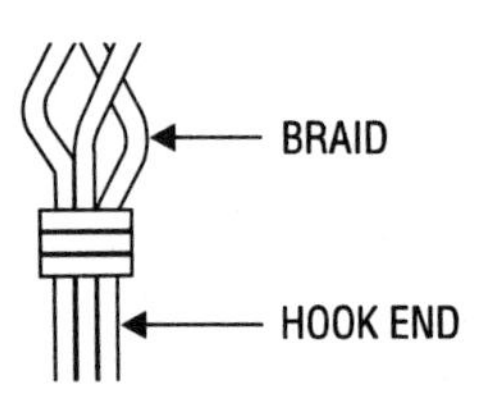

Diagram 64

R. Using other 3" wrap wire, wrap it around wires at end of braid. (Also make sure **ENDS** of **THIS** wrap wire on same side of bracelet as ends of wrap wire at other end of bracelet.) Hook end of bracelet should now look like *Diagram 64.*

S. Using wide nose pliers, grasp last 1/4" of all three wires (at same time) and fold them over. *Diagram 65*

T. Using wide nose pliers, or needle nose pliers, bend wires again as shown in *Diagram 66.*

U. The bracelet can now be shaped easily by using wide nose pliers. Bend bracelet every 1/4" along its entire length in same direction. Feed bracelet into jaws of pliers (perpendicular to them) and push gently down with thumb. Be sure to do this entire length of bracelet, including hook and loop at either end.

Diagram 65

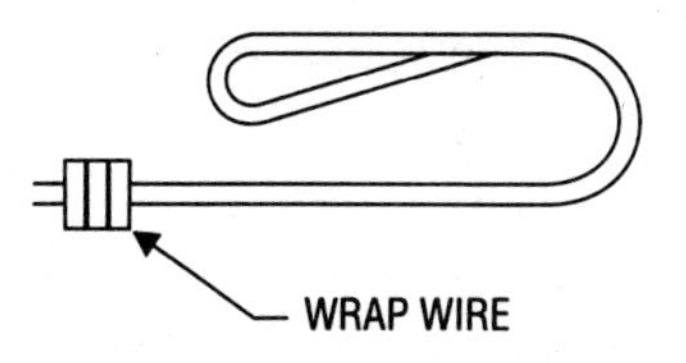

Diagram 66

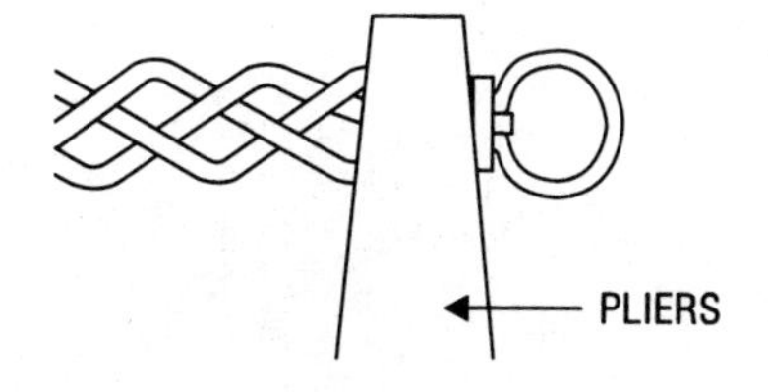

Diagram 67

The variety of the particular style is as infinite as one's imagination. Following are a few suggestions. Just remember, the technique for all of them is the same as described in Steps A through U (with some noted exceptions.)

1. Three wire braided with 4mm beads every 1/2" on center wire.

2. Three wire braided: two gold and one silver or vice-versa.

3. Six wire braided (using three groups of two wires each.)

4. Nine wire braids (using three groups of three wires each.)

5. Twelve wire twisted braided (using three groups of four wires each.)

Remember, do not hesitate to mix gold and silver wires. The effect can be stunning, especially when it is twisted. Bracelets with more than three wires are fun.

Just remember you need three groups of wires. *Diagram 68* which follows is self explanatory.

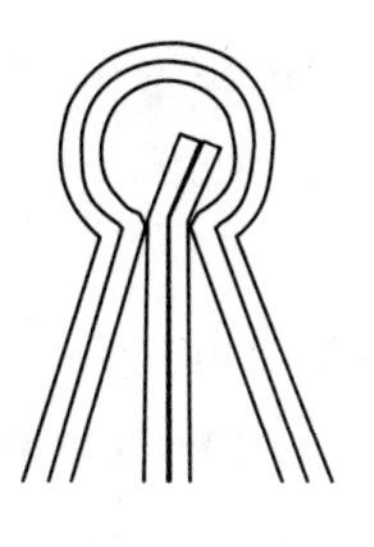

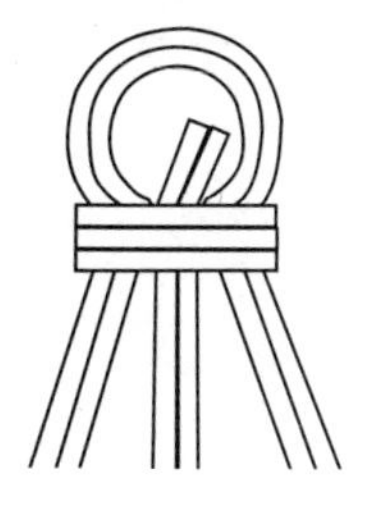

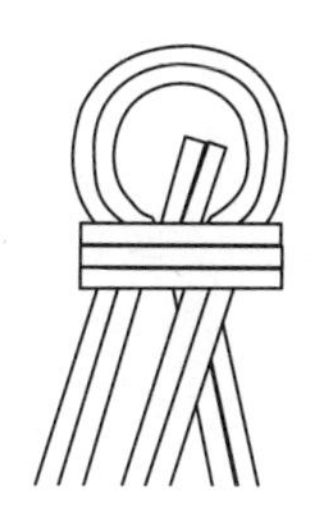

6 WIRES

9 WIRES

Diagram 68

Diagram 69: Example of nine wire braided bracelet: (Use same procedure for 6, 9, and 12 wire braided bracelet.)

Follow steps S and T to make the hook end.

There are many other systems for making bracelet fasteners, but what is shown here is simple and easy to do. It has worked well for me.

Diagram 69

#2 STANDARD FORM BRACELET

A. Attempt to make this bracelet only if you are totally familiar with Standard Form Ring system.

B. Use a minimum of 12 wires (square 20 gauge and a 30mm x 40mm cabochon.)

C. Follow same procedure you would for making a Standard Form Ring except **THINK BIG!!!!** Follow instructions A through O on pages 42-46 with a few modifications which are only understood if you are familiar with mechanics of wirewrapping.

D. Use measurement found on page 47, number 5 or 6.

E. Use a glass to bend wire around (minimum of 2" in diameter.)

F. Stone will be mounted with longer dimension **ACROSS** wrist, perpendicular to fingers.

G. Cut wrapwires at least 6" long.

H. After wires are bent in U shape, wrap wires must be moved down so when cradle wires are bent up, they will easily accommodate stone. See Step G on page 43 for this procedure. Wrap wires must be pushed down a lot more than what was done for Standard Form Ring.

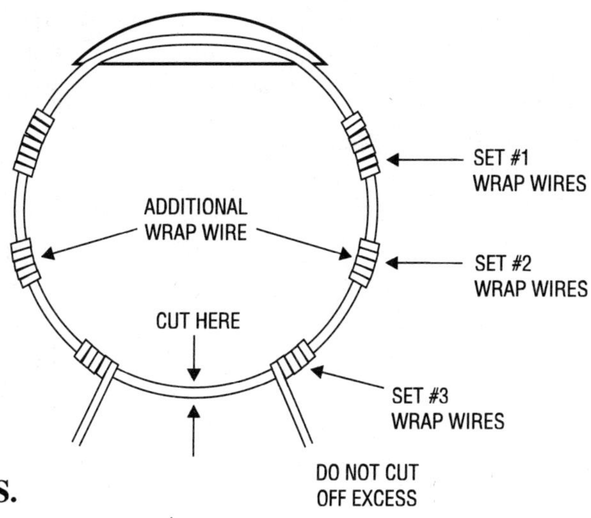

Diagram 70

I. When stone is mounted you will have one giant size Standard Form Ring; **PLEASE NOTE INSTRUCTIONS WITH DIAGRAMS.**

AFTER THIRD SET OF WRAP WIRES ARE ADDED, CUT SHANK WIRES EXACTLY MIDWAY BETWEEN THEM AND WITH WIDE NOSE PLIERS, FOLD BACK ENDS AS INDICATED.

Now use excess wrap wires to cover ends of shank wires. *Diagram 71*

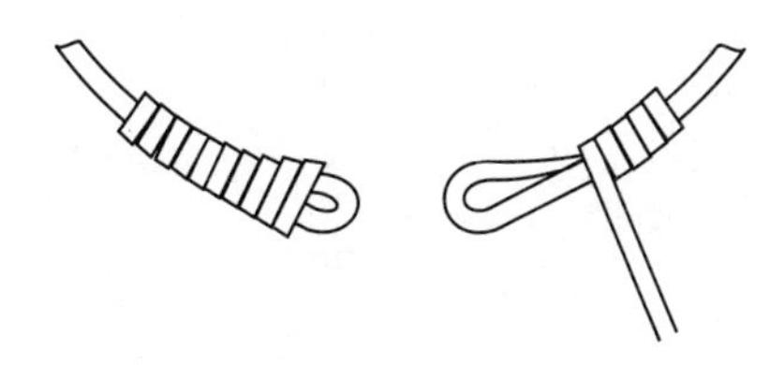

Diagram 71

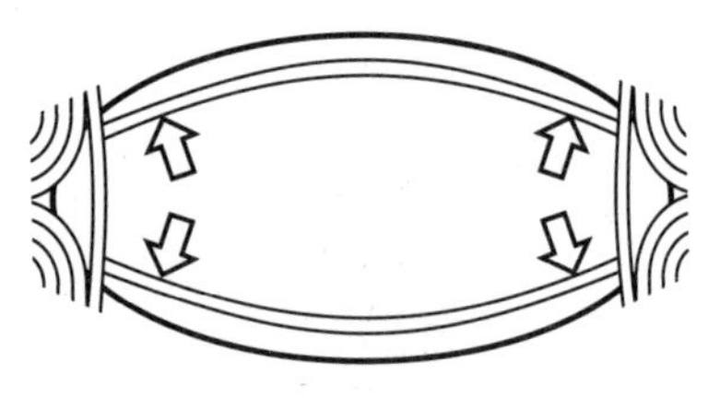

TOP VIEW
BEFORE

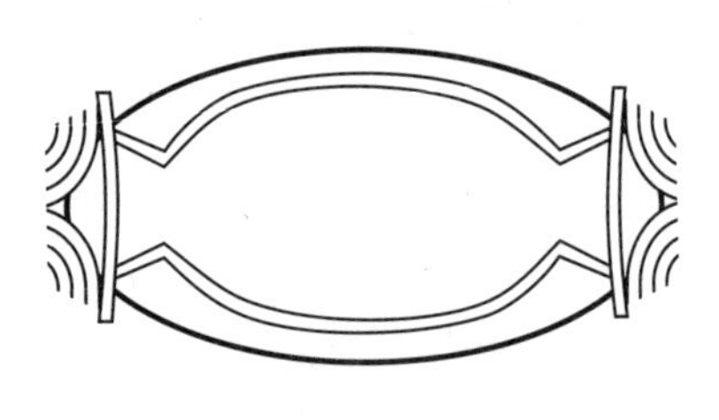

TOP VIEW
AFTER

Diagram 72

J. After shank wires have been cut at bottom, cradle wires holding the stone have a tendency to loosen. This slack can be taken up (easily) using wide nose pliers.

K. Grip each cradle wire at arrows and twist inward. Do same at other arrows. *Diagram 72*

If necessary, do likewise to bottom cradle wire or just one good twist in middle.

#1 BIRD CAGE EARRINGS

A. Cut two wires 8" long (21 gauge square).

B. Bend each in opposite direction as shown. *Diagram 73*

Bird Cage Earrings

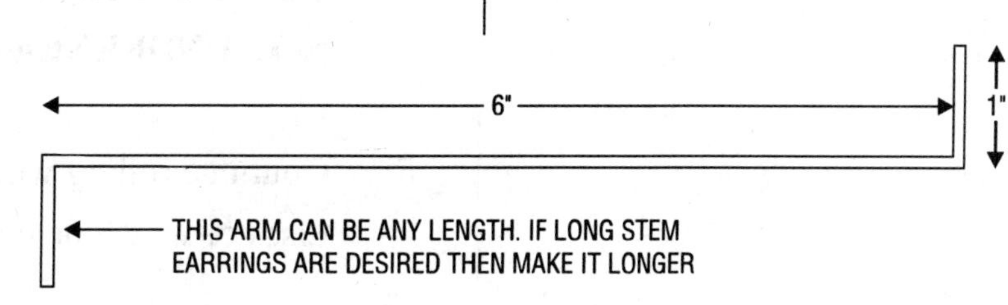

Diagram 73

C. Using needle nose pliers, grip wire so end of 1" length is pointing towards hand holding pliers. Bend 6" wire around one tip of needle nose pliers as shown. *Diagram 74*

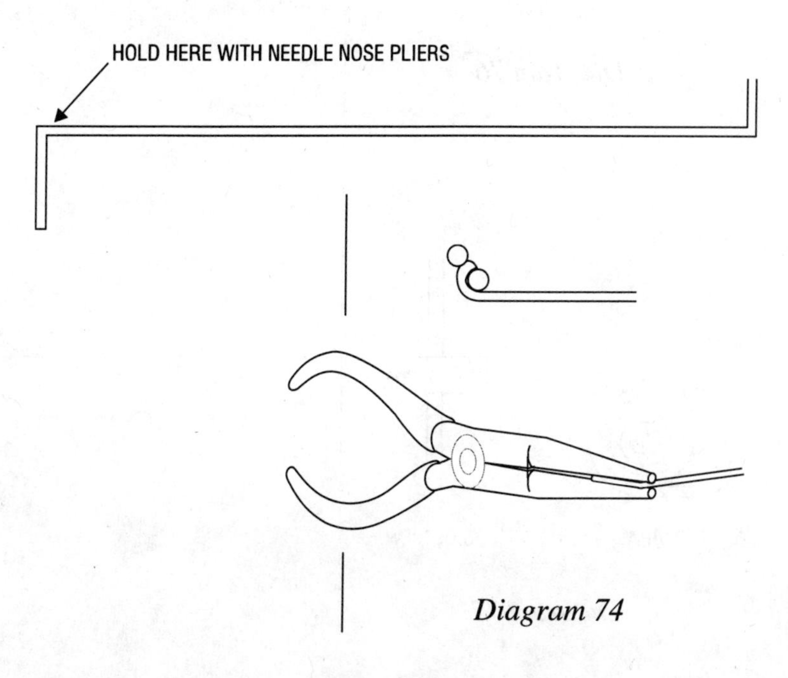

Diagram 74

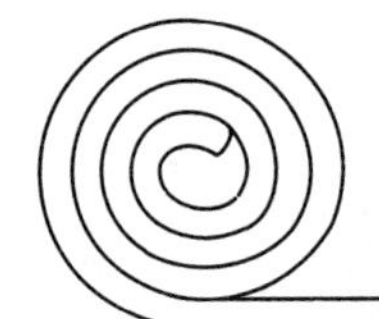

D. Continue bending wire into disk as shown (using wide nose pliers).

Diagram 75

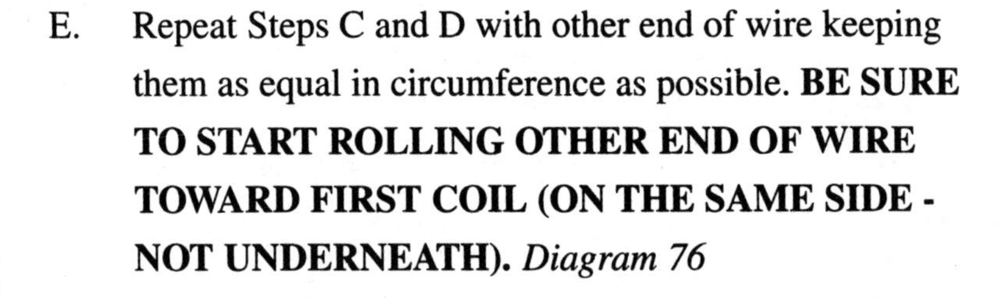

E. Repeat Steps C and D with other end of wire keeping them as equal in circumference as possible. **BE SURE TO START ROLLING OTHER END OF WIRE TOWARD FIRST COIL (ON THE SAME SIDE - NOT UNDERNEATH).** *Diagram 76*

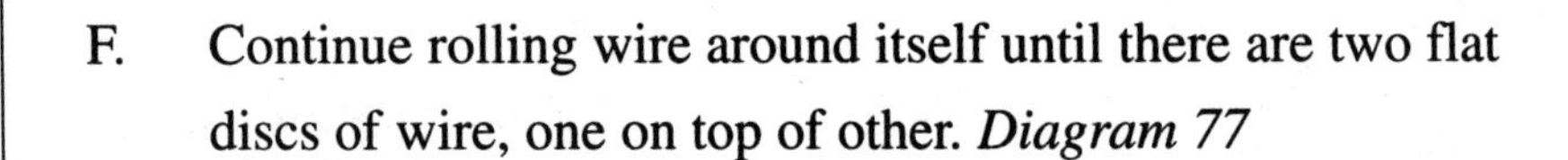

F. Continue rolling wire around itself until there are two flat discs of wire, one on top of other. *Diagram 77*

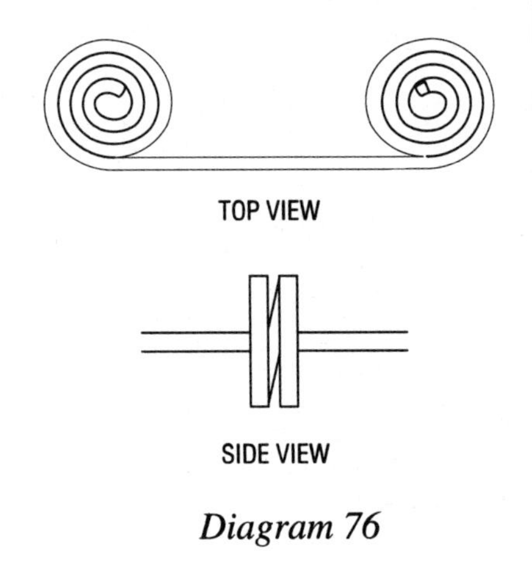

Diagram 76

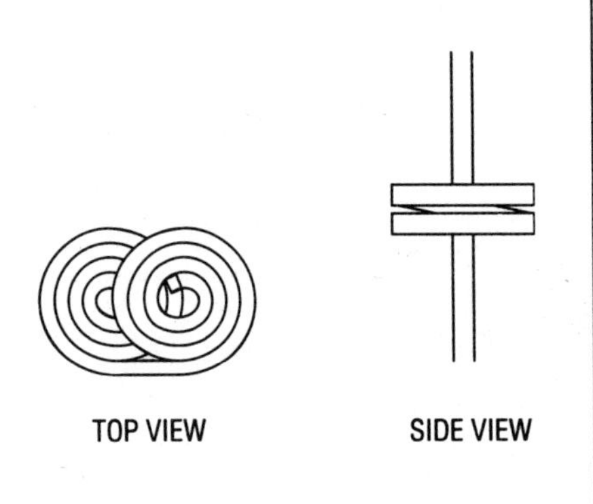

Diagram 77

G. Very gently, pull flat wire discs apart. Hold one end of wire with pliers and using thumb and forefinger of other hand, pull downward, gently, then turn bird cage over and do likewise with other side. There will be minor bendings and shaping adjustments to be made with wide nose pliers. Do not let opening between wires get so large it cannot hold a small stone. Bird cage should now look like *Diagram 78.*

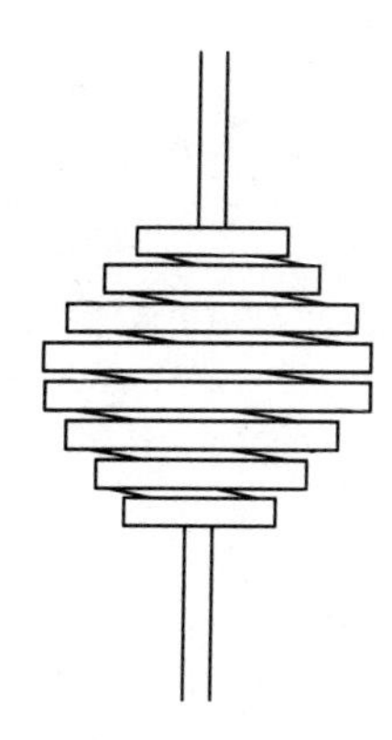

Diagram 78

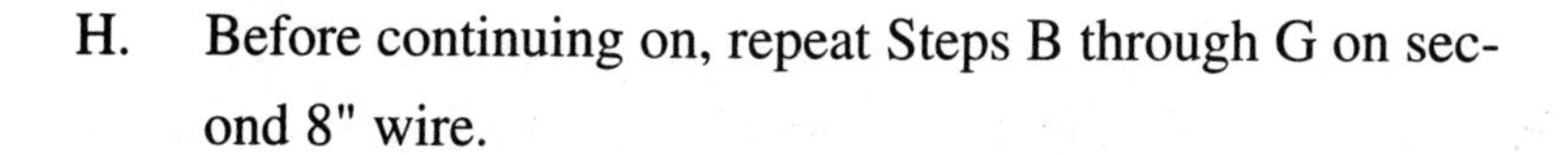

H. Before continuing on, repeat Steps B through G on second 8" wire.

I. You now have two similar bird cages (it is impossible to make them absolutely identical so don't waste time trying). Cut off bottom wire of each bird cage.

J. Decide on length of stem desired, measure and cut off both bird cages and put a loop in both. *Diagram 79* (This loop is for insertion of an earwire or it can be put on a clamp type fastener.)

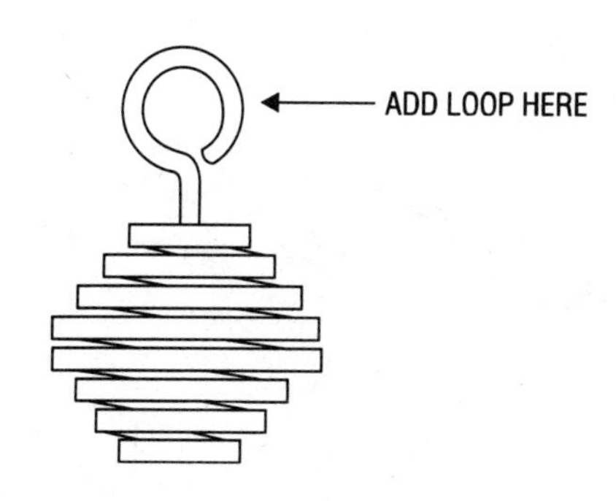

Diagram 79

K. Spread bird cage in middle and insert small stone, then close bird cage with pliers. It is important stone be longer than it is wide.

L. For larger earrings use longer piece of wire. To accommodate larger stones, start coil of wire on larger part of jaws of needle nose pliers.

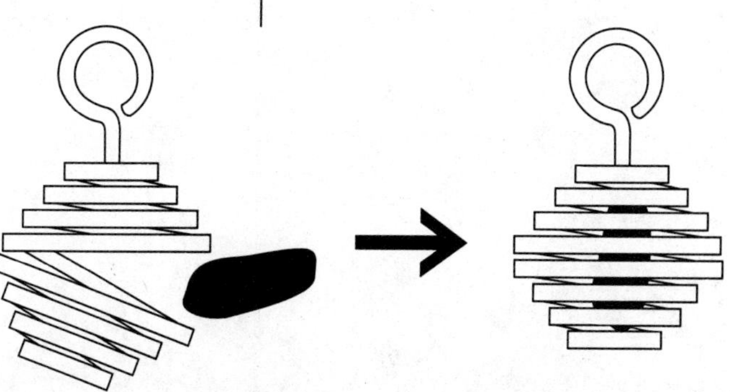

Diagram 80

#2 EARRING VARIATIONS

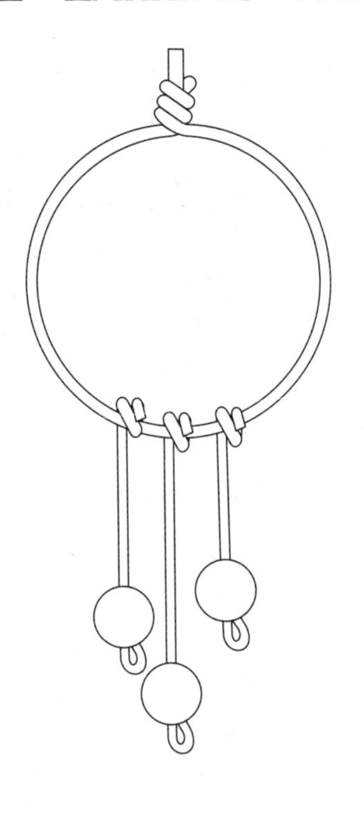

A. Follow same directions for three wire bracelet except use 22 gauge wire and make it no larger than circumference of a 25 cent piece. Also use three (4mm) beads spaced evenly. Also, no clasp is necessary - use center wire to fasten neatly together. Left over center wire can be used as stem for ear wire also.

B. Many variations of plain wire, bent in variety of shapes can be used.

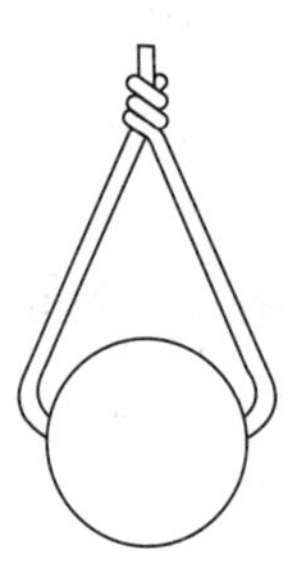
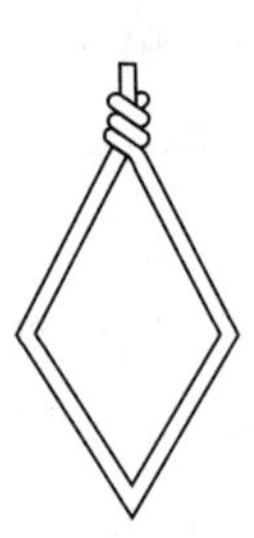
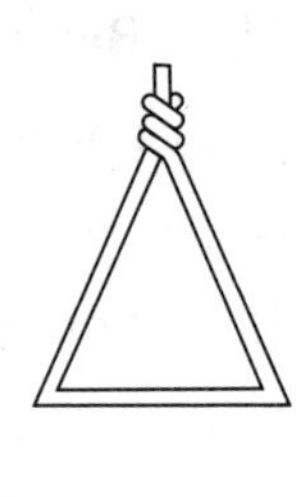

All Wire Pendant
Cross
Double Wire
Shark's Tooth
Double Wire
Pendant
Single Wire Pendant Variations
Double Stone
Pendant
Shark's Tooth
Pendant
Bird Cage Earrings
Shark's Tooth
Pendant
Earring Variations
Moods In Wire™

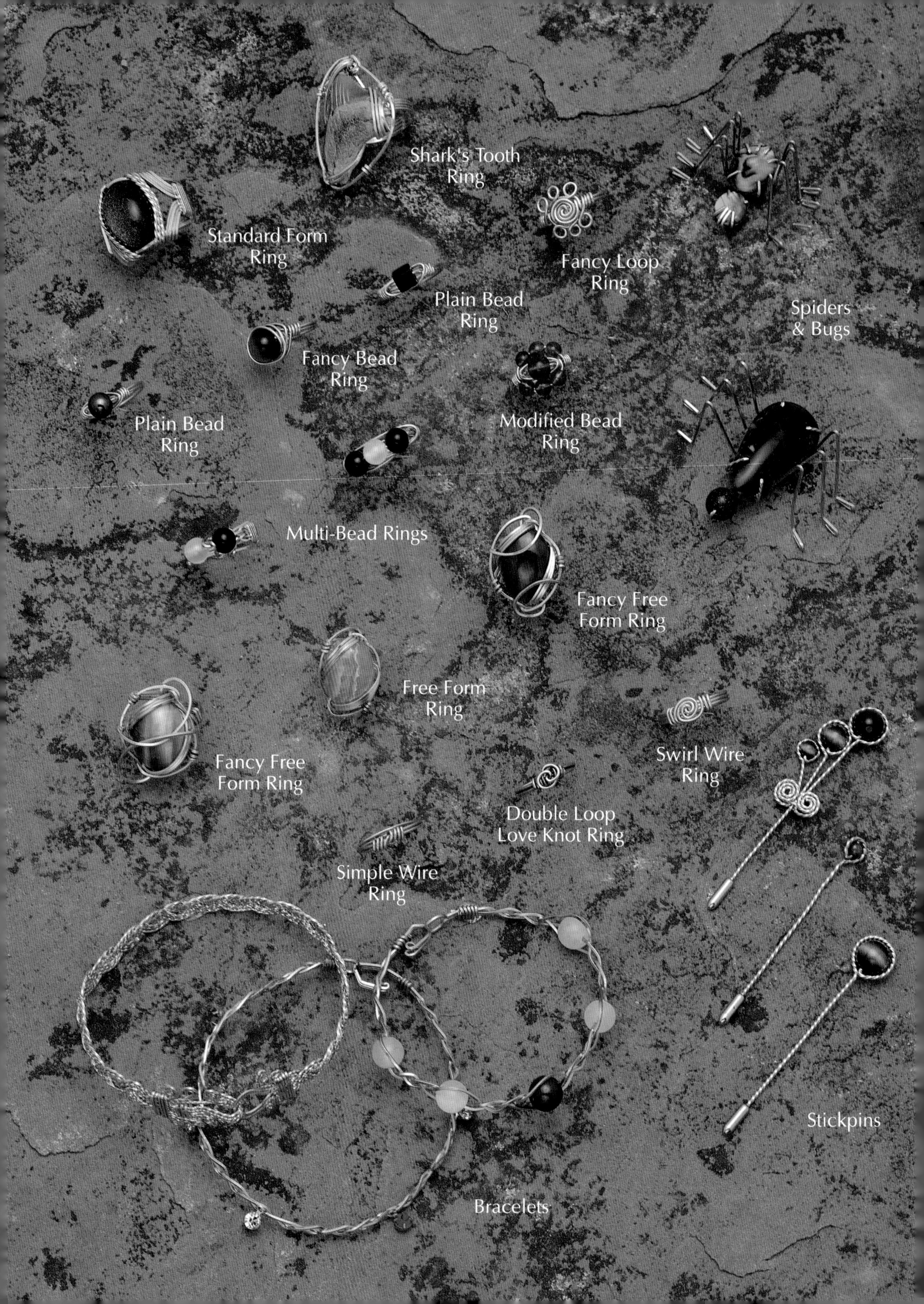
Shark's Tooth
Ring
Standard Form
Ring
Fancy Loop
Ring
Plain Bead
Ring
Spiders
& Bugs
Fancy Bead
Ring
Plain Bead
Ring
Modified Bead
Ring
Multi-Bead Rings
Fancy Free
Form Ring
Free Form
Ring
Swirl Wire
Ring
Fancy Free
Form Ring
Double Loop
Love Knot Ring
Simple Wire
Ring
Stickpins
Bracelets

#1 SINGLE WIRE PENDANT

This is a system by which any stone, regardless of size or shape can be securely anchored (quickly) in wire first and then wrapped creatively with remaining wire. As a personal preference I use this system mostly on baroque (tumbled) stones and odd shaped cabochons. Flat, odd shaped slabs are ideal. Cut stones, as well as faceted stones of any size and shape can be used. (Marquise and oval cabochons, when wrapped with this system look absolutely stunning.)

See cover & photo insert for variations of the Single Wire Pendant.

For the following (diagrammed, step by step) instructions, I have used a small flat baroque slab 2-1/4" long and a single piece of 20 gauge round, gold-filled (14kt) wire about 16" long. I use round wire almost exclusively for this system. It is easier to use and eliminates other problems typical of square wire - keeping it flat, etc. I do use square wire only after it is twisted. Below you will find a chart which will be helpful and is self explanatory. These wire lengths are long for a reason you will discover!

Single Wire Pendants

Stone Size	Wire Gauge	Wire Length
3/4" to 1-1/2"	22 to 21 Round	9" to 13"
1-1/2" to 2-1/2"	21 to 20 Round	14" to 16"
2" to 4"	2 strands of 22 Round	16" to 20" to 24"
20mm x 30mm Cabs	20 Round	16" to 18"
Small Earrings: 8mm x 10mm or 10mm x 14mm	22 Round	4" to 8"
30mm x 40mm Cabs	2 strands of 22 or 1 strand of 21	20" to 24"

The most important aspect of this system is persistence and imagination. The designs are truly infinite. If a wire breaks, the design must be altered to continue on. At the end of this section there will be illustrations to stimulate your own initiative. This system requires boldness and aggressiveness in using the wires. Do not get mired down in trying to make decisions. This can only lead to frustration. Relax and enjoy! If you are new to wirewrapping, it may be a good idea to get a coil of copper or brass wire with which to practice.

A. Select a small flat baroque stone no longer than 2-1/4" and less than 1" wide at its widest point. Also, at either end it should (but not necessarily) come to a narrow point. *Diagram 81.* **IMPORTANT...DECIDE WHICH IS TO BE THE TOP, BOTTOM, FRONT, AND BACK.**

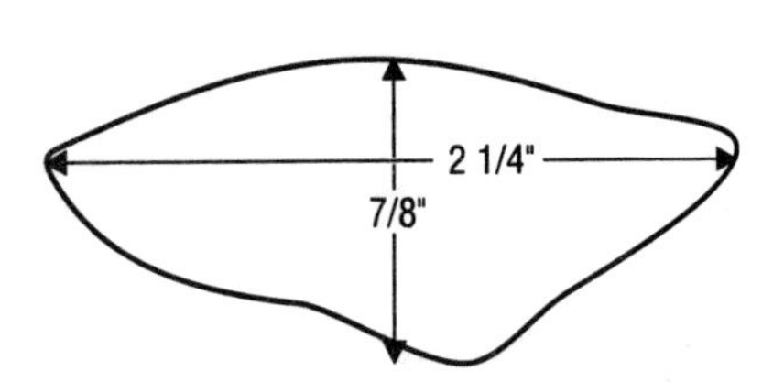

Diagram 81

B. Cut a piece of 20 gauge round wire 16" long. Clean wire by gripping one end of it with wide nose pliers and pulling it through a jewelers cloth several times, and at the same time, try to straighten it a much as possible.

C. Find middle of wire and place wire on back of stone **KEEPING IN MIND WHICH IS TOP, WHICH IS BOTTOM, FRONT, AND BACK**. Make sure there is equal length of wire at top and bottom of stone.

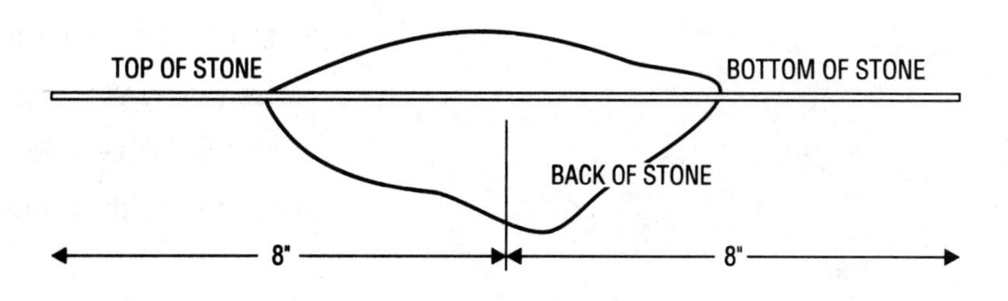

Diagram 82

D. Using wide nose pliers, bend wire as shown. *Diagram 83*

E. Holding stone and wire in right hand and pressing down with right thumb on top of wire at 90 degree bend, use left forefinger and hand to wrap wire completely around stone as tight as possible.

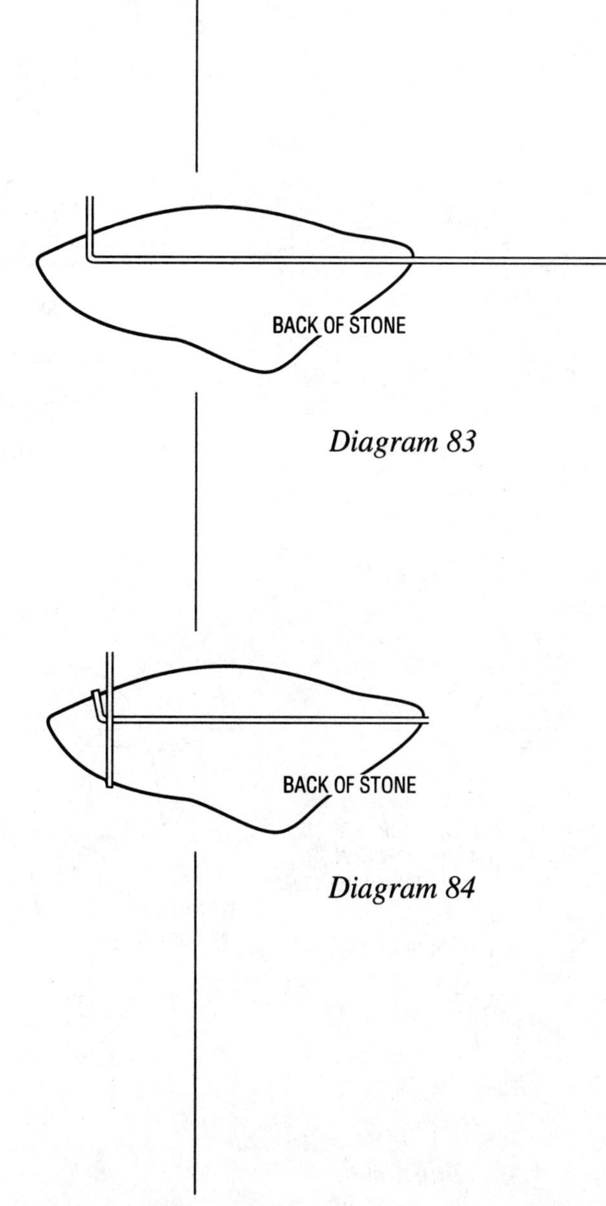

Diagram 83

Diagram 84

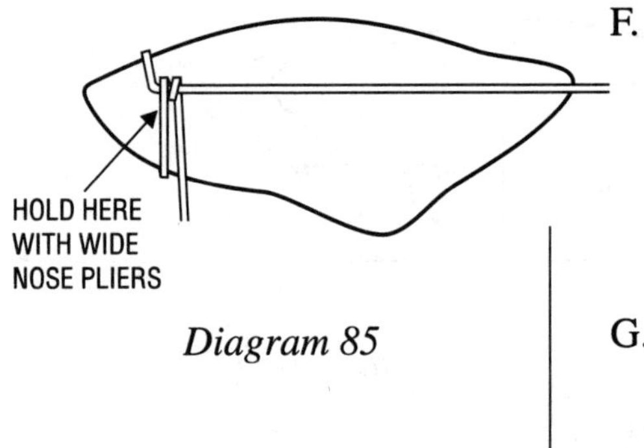

Diagram 85

F. Remove stone and holding loop in place with wide nose pliers (very, very tightly as indicated in *Diagram 85*), wrap wire (that goes around stone) one and a half times around wire that runs full length of stone.

G. Reinsert same end of stone in completed loop making sure back, front, top, and bottom is as planned in Step C.

H. Repeat Steps D through G at other end of stone. It should now look like *Diagram 86*

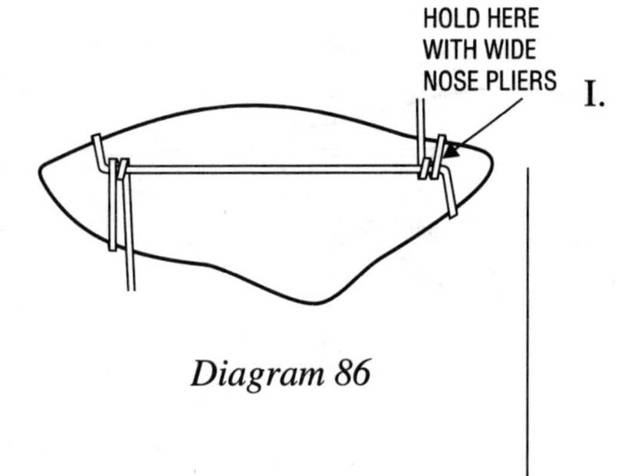

Diagram 86

I. Grip wire that runs the length of the back of stone with wide nose pliers and turn clockwise about 1/4" turn **or less**. Do it slowly, but not tight enough to break wire. This will tighten loops around end of stone and lock wire onto stone too. Grip wire in shaded area as shown. *Diagram 87*

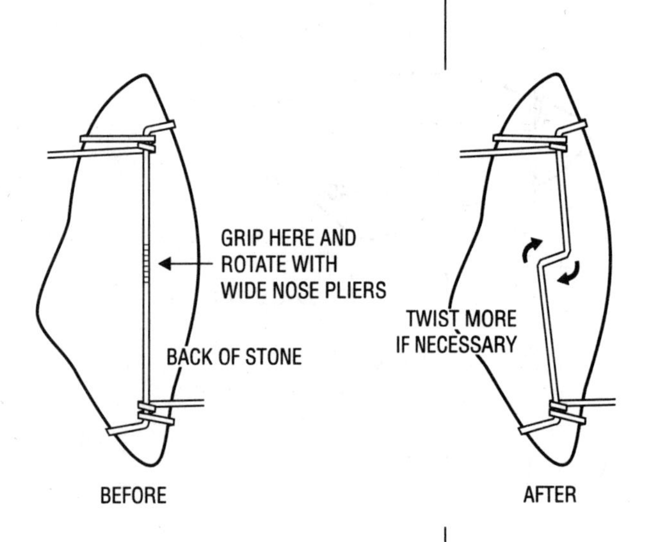

Diagram 87

J. Take remaining wire at top of stone and bend it in an arc to your left, bringing it across front face of stone a little bit better than half way up from bottom of stone and bend it around and across back of stone exactly where wire begins to cross face of stone. *Diagram 88*

K. Bottom wire can be bent as shown and secured to wires on back.

L. To give added support to wide loops around stone, other wires can be added. These wires must be anchored to wire running down the back of stone. *Diagram 89*

M. This is only one suggestion as to how to wrap remaining wire around stone. There are many variations. When you feel confident, try something different. Be adventurous. You will discover the shape of stone will play a major part in design.

FOR A BROACH: If a broach is desired, simply incorporate an extra (twisted, square) wire in the beginning and make it into a pin. This extra wire can also be added later.

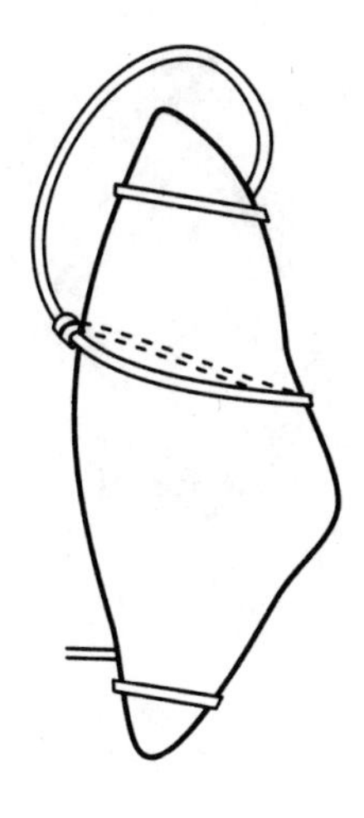

Diagram 88

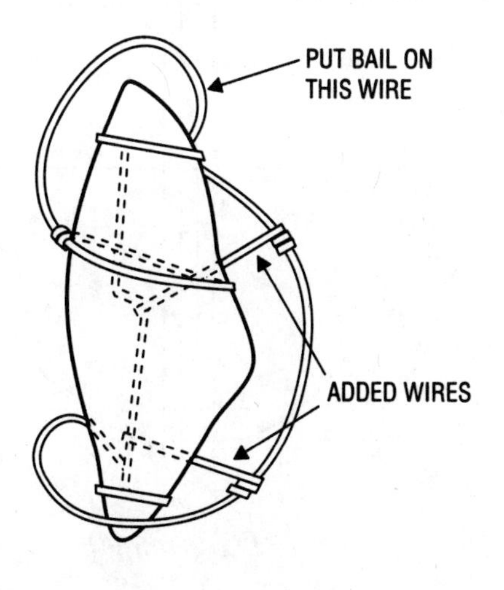

Diagram 89

#2 THREE WIRE PENDANT

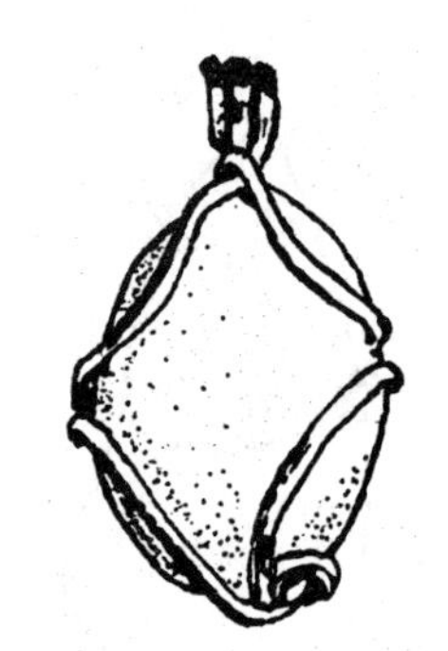

Three Wire Pendant

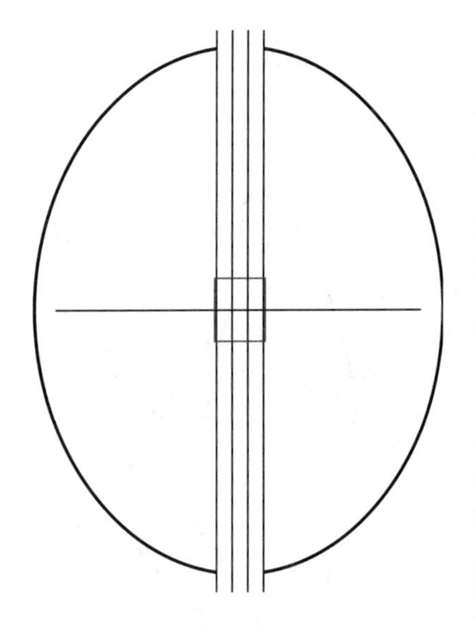

Diagram 90

A. Cut three wires 8" long (20 gauge square).

B. Cut two wires 3" long (20 gauge square).

C. Select a 30mm x 40mm cabochon.

D. Put a piece of masking tape around three 8" wires at center. Mark exact halfway point of 8" wires.

E. Mark center of stone also (halfway between 40mm length).

F. Place center wire mark of taped wires on center mark of cabochon. *Diagram 90*

G. With red felt tip pen, mark wires at edge of stone.

H. With two 3" wires, wrap one each where it has been marked. Make sure wraps are made in direction toward center of stone.

I. Make sure wrap wires do not extend beyond outer edge of cabochon. (The ends of wrap wires should be turned toward stone.) Remove tape. *Diagram 91*

J. Hold cabochon and wire firmly in left hand. Wires should be held across fingertips with cabochon on top, and thumb on top of stone. **IT IS ABSOLUTELY IMPERATIVE WIRES BE HELD STRAIGHT THE FULL LENGTH OF CABOCHON. DO NOT LET THEM TILT TO ONE SIDE.**

K. Bend left hand wire down across face of stone, pull it to right of center as shown. *Diagram 92*

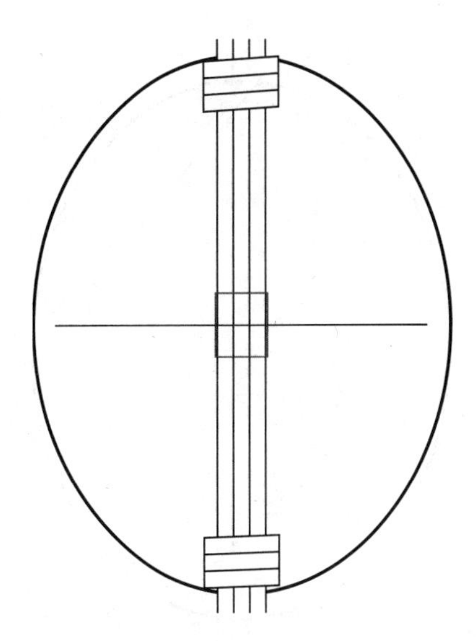

Diagram 91

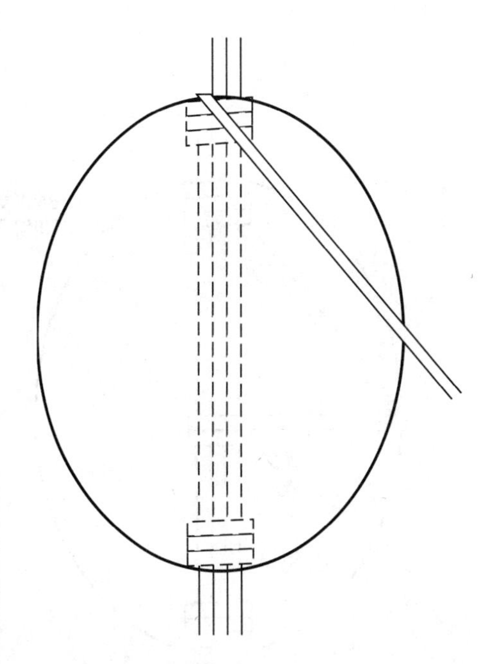

Diagram 92

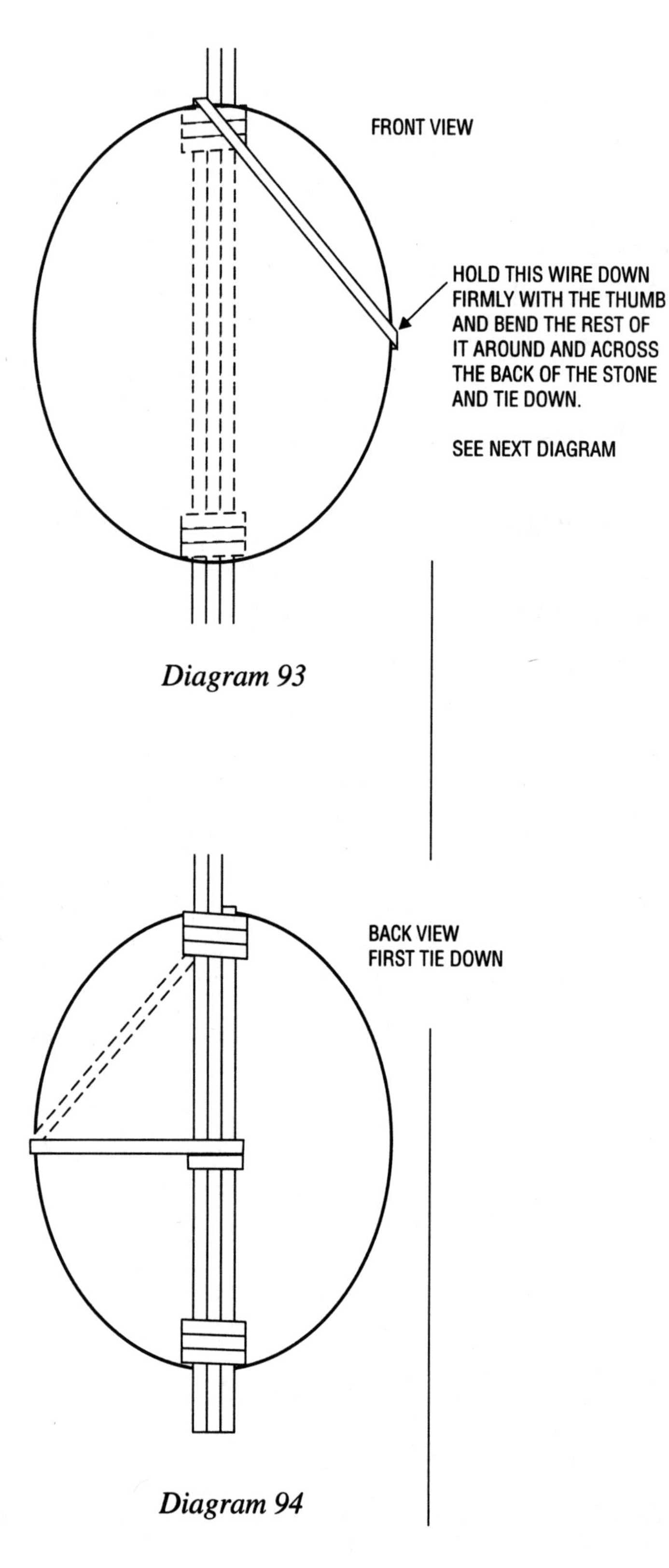

Diagram 93

Diagram 94

L. Bend same wire around to back of stone at halfway mark so it can be tied to wires on back of stone. *Diagram 93*

Hold wire down firmly with thumb and bend the rest of it around and across back of stone and tie down. *Diagram 94*

M. Repeat Steps J through L for remaining wires. The wire that is diagonally across from first wire tie down should be next. *Diagram 95*

After tying down second wire, stone is now secure. The other two wires can be bent into position and tied down easily.

N. Repeat process for remaining two wires. Please keep in mind symmetry of design. *Diagram 96*

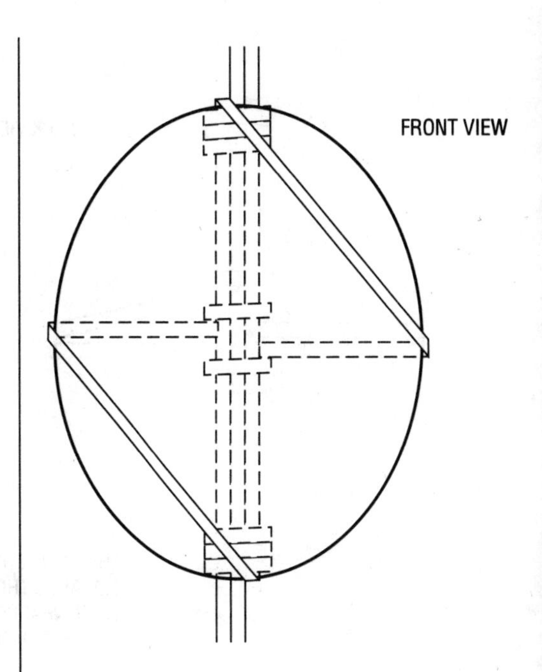

Diagram 95

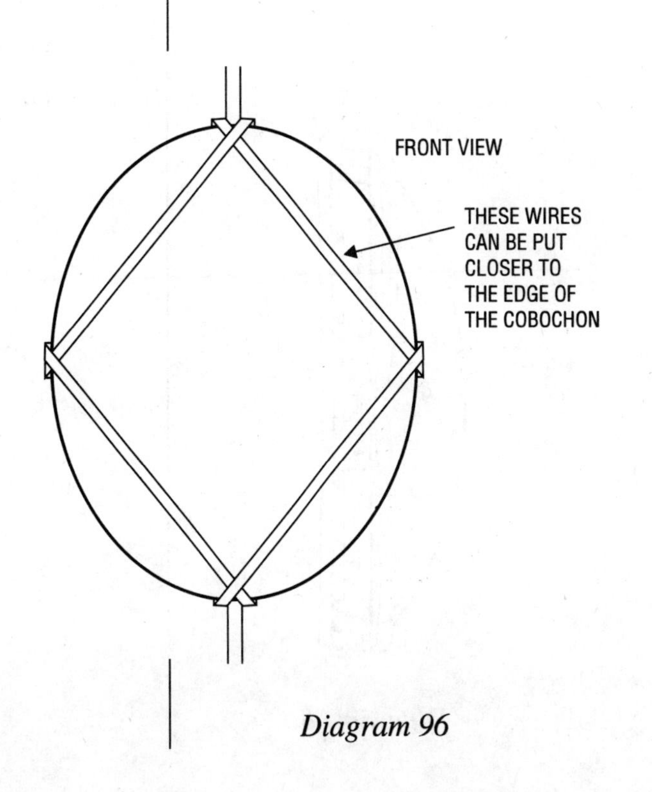

Diagram 96

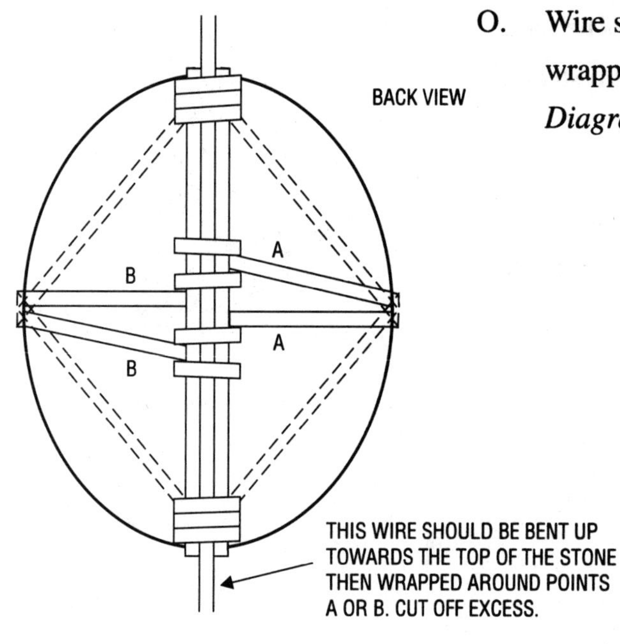

Diagram 97

O. Wire should be bent up towards top of stone then wrapped around points A or B and excess cut off. *Diagram 97*

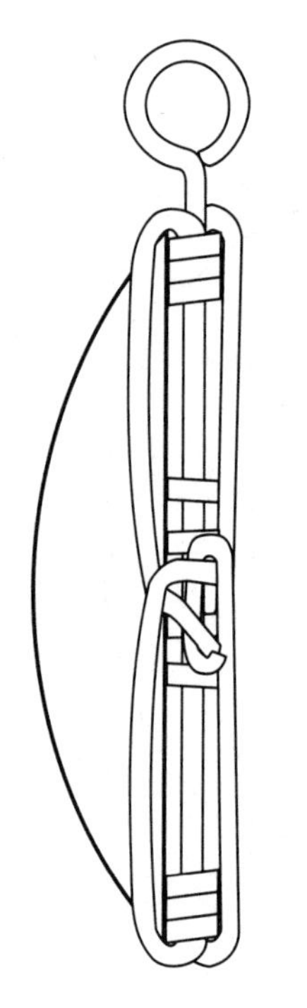

Diagram 98

P. Using needle nose pliers, roll a loop using remaining center wire at top. Make sure loop is large enough to put a chain through. See side view of *Diagram 98.*

#3 "CLASSIC PENDANT"

(All measurements are for 30mm x 40mm cabochon.)

Classic Pendant

A. Cut four wires 8-1/2" long. Cut two wires 4" long. Cut one wire 5" long. Cut one wire 3" long. (ALL WIRE IS 20 GAUGE SQUARE)

B. Using pin vise, twist two of 8-1/2" wires and 3" wire.

C. Bend over 1/4" one end of 4" and 5" wires and wrap around group wires making sure the 5" wire is in center of 8-1/2" wires. **MAKE SURE TWISTED WIRES ARE IN MIDDLE OF GROUP WIRES.** Use *Diagram 99* for placement and measurement.

DO NOT CUT OFF EXCESS WRAP WIRE

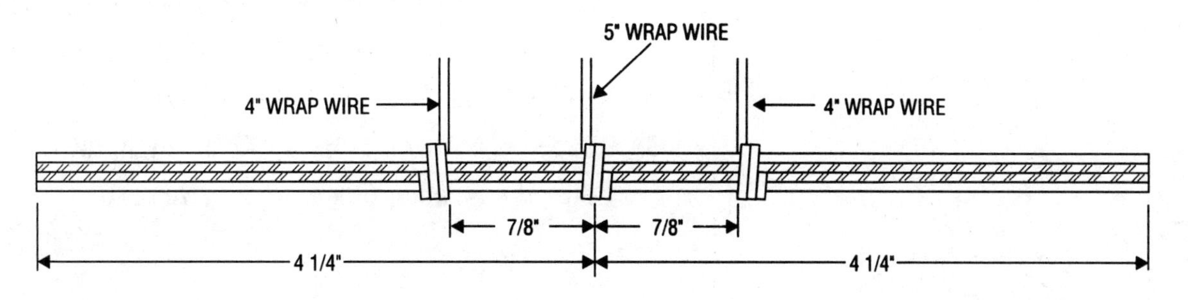

Diagram 99

D. **IT IS IMPERATIVE THAT WRAP WIRES BE PUT ON AS SHOWN. ALL ENDS ARE TO BE ON SAME SIDE OF GROUP WIRES.**

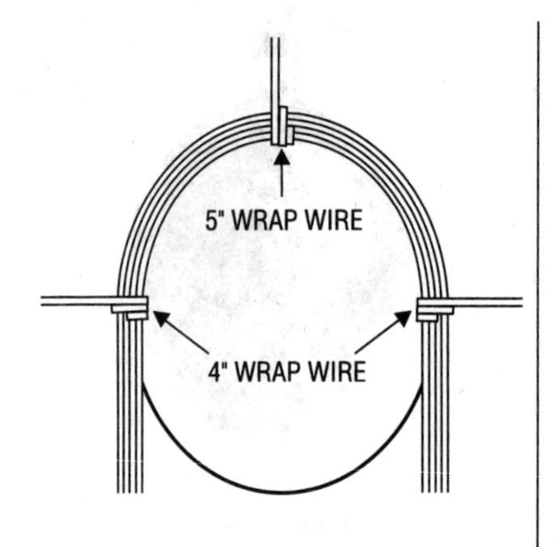

Diagram 100

E. After all wrap wires are on, bend group wires as shown. Bend them very slowly and gently, keeping them between thumb and forefinger of each hand. To make it easier, hold wires in center with wide nose pliers and bend (very gently) one side at a time. **BEND VERY SLOWLY TO AVOID WARP OR OTHER DISTORTIONS BROUGHT ON BY BENDING FOUR WIRES TOGETHER SIMULTANEOUSLY. ALSO, MAKE SURE THEY ARE KEPT FLAT WHILE BENDING.** *Diagram 100*

The group wires should follow contour of outer edge of stone, overlapping it slightly.

F. Using 3" twisted wire, form into circle small enough to fit on back of cabochon. Wrap ends very tightly around each other so it becomes a permanent circle. This will be the anchor wire to which all other wires will be tied.

G. Tape anchor wire to back of cabochon, toward top and directly in center of stone. *Diagram 101*

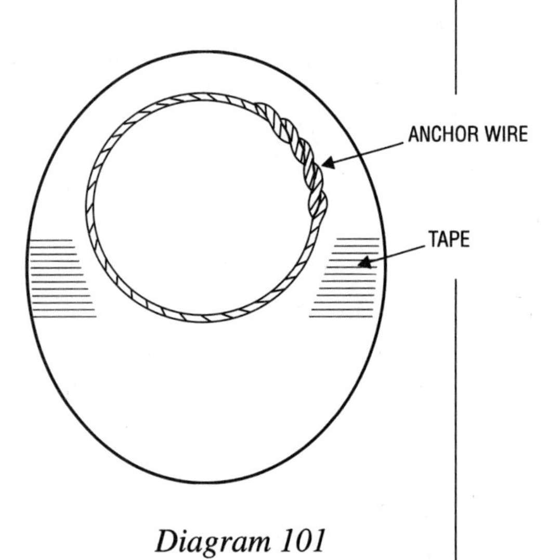

Diagram 101

H. Using thick part of needle nose pliers, make triple loop in center wrap wire as shown in front and side views in *Diagram 102 & 103.*

I. Other two 4" wrap wires must also be bent and tied to anchor wire as shown. Be sure to leave 1/2" excess wire in case more adjustments are needs. *Diagram 104*

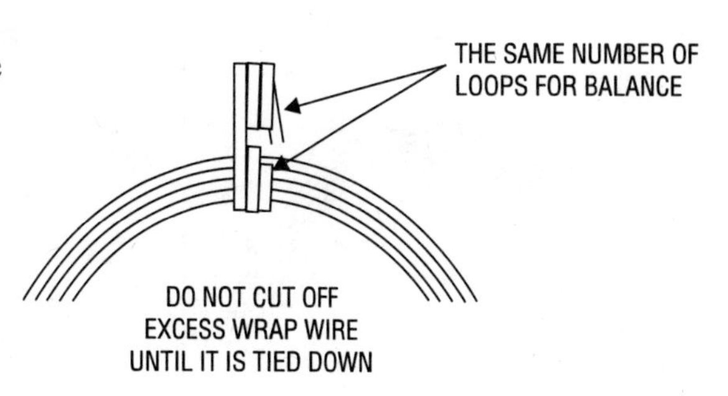

Diagram 102

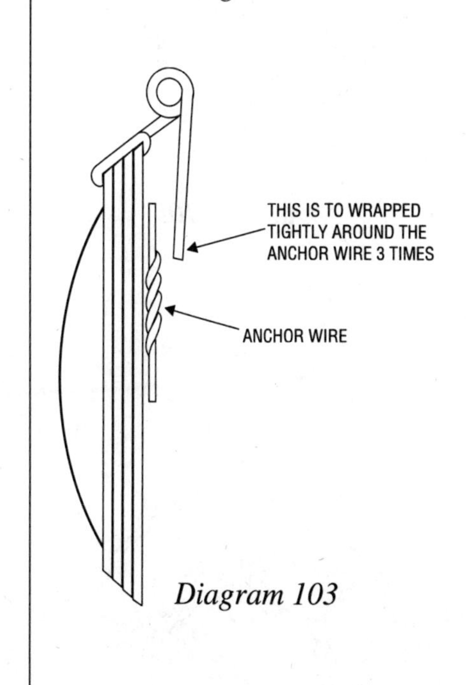

Diagram 103

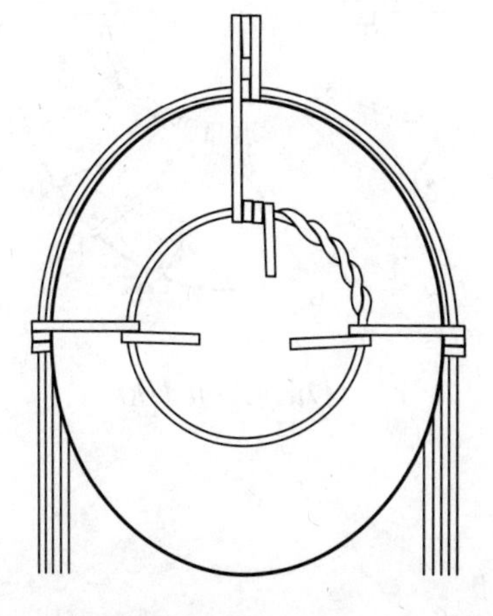

Diagram 104

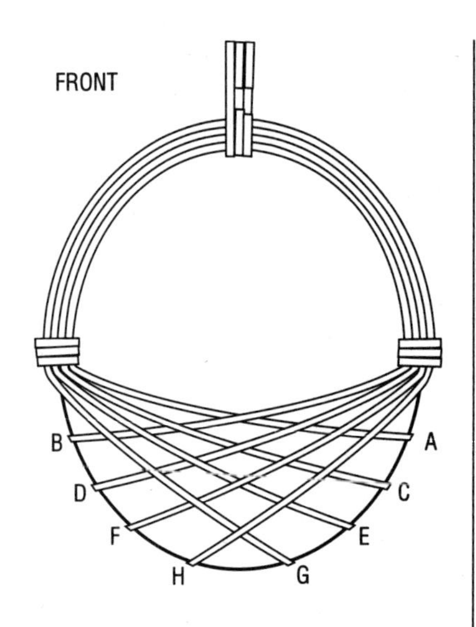

Diagram 105

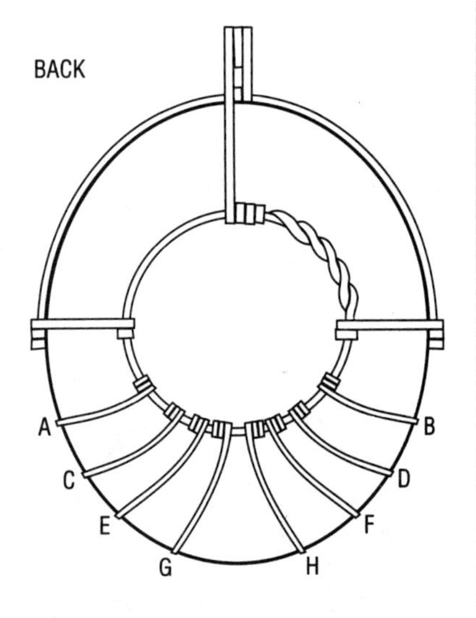

Diagram 106

J. Turn stone face up and proceed to bend around and tie down to anchor wire, from left to right the following:

First Wire:	A	Fifth Wire:	E
Second:	B	Sixth:	F
Third:	C	Seventh:	G
Fourth:	D	Eighth:	H

Diagrams 105 & 106 should be self-explanatory.

All tie downs are tucked under anchor wire. File any rough edges.

#4 PLAIN ALL WIRE PENDANT

A. Cut three wires, 20 gauge square 8" long. Do not straighten wires. Let natural curvature (of coil from which they were cut) remain.

B. Cut three wrap wires 4" long, bend over one end of each 1/2".

C. With wide nose pliers, bend each of 8" wires exactly at halfway point. Bend them, one at a time, approximately 120 degrees. **BE SURE BEND IS IN SAME DIRECTION AS NATURAL CURVATURE OF THE WIRE.** *Diagram 107*

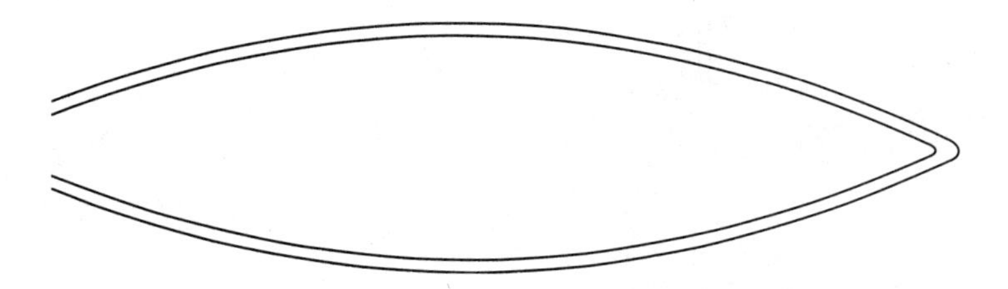

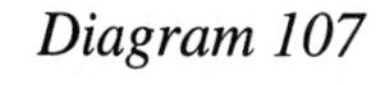

Diagram 107

D. After all three wires are bent, put them together with wrap wires a indicated. Make sure wrap wire ends are all on same side of pendant. It is arbitrary where "tail" of "fish" comes together. Keep in mind pendant looks better if body of fish is long and narrow.

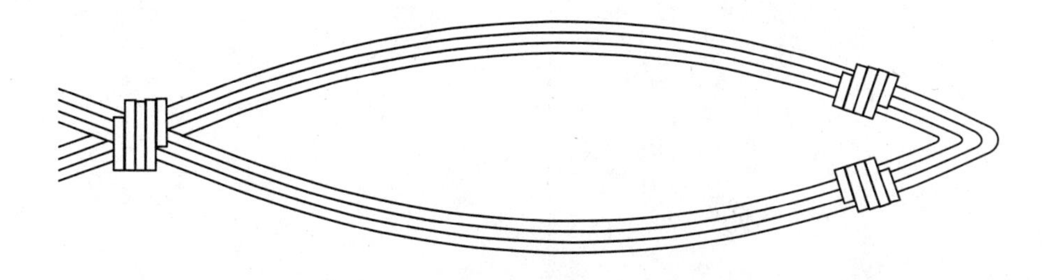

Diagram 108

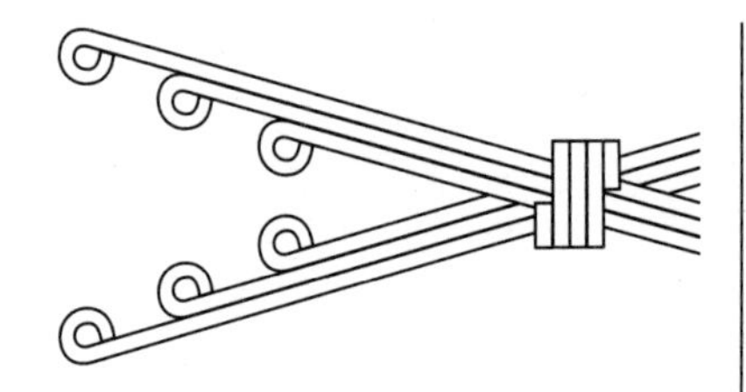

Diagram 109

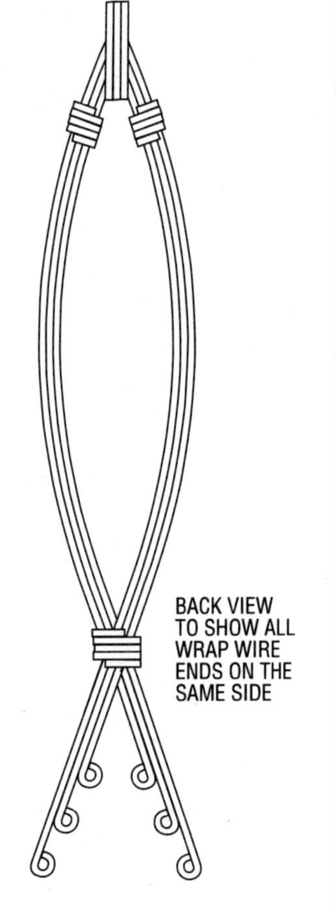

Diagram 110

E. Ends of wires are uneven. They may be finished off as the diagram suggests. Tail of fish may be spread farther apart so as to give a better effect.

F. A bail can be put on top of pendant and can be suspended from a chain as indicated in *Diagram 110.*

#1 BIRD NEST BEAD STICKPINS

Materials: One 6mm drilled bead
One 8" length of 22 gauge round wire
One 5" length of 20 gauge square wire
One clutch

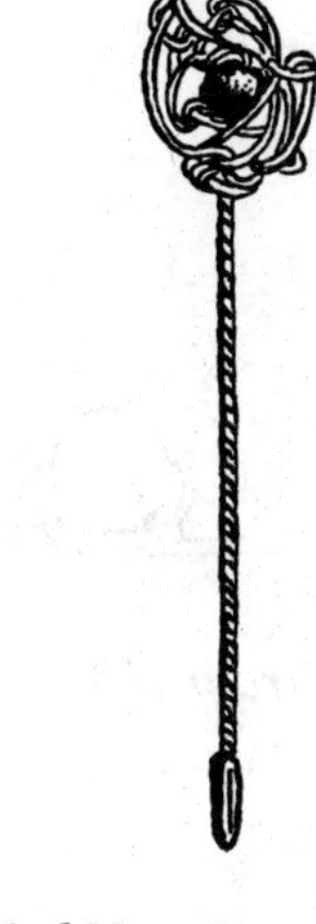

Bird Nest Bead Stickpin

A. Put one end of wire in side of vise and tighten. Now put bead on it and move bead to halfway point.

B. Take right end of wire (do not remove from vise yet) and make loop around bead, keeping loop and bead as near halfway (4") length as possible. Loop can be moved back and forth after free end of wire is put through it to form a knot. Pull tight with wide nose pliers. *Diagram 112*

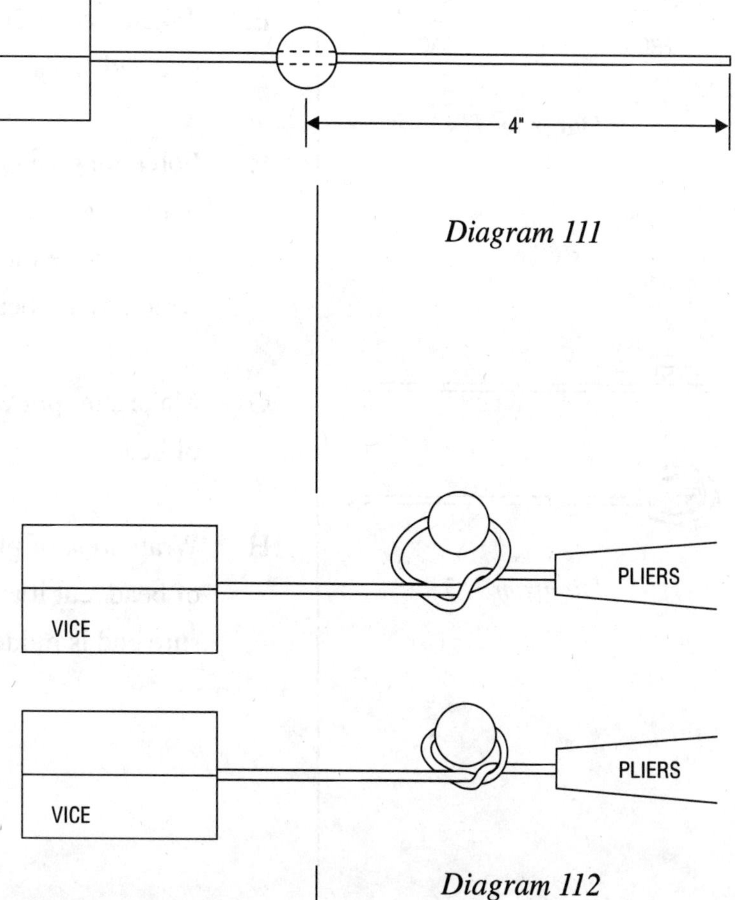

Diagram 111

Diagram 112

C. With one end of wire still in vise, make another loop over bead. Put end of wire through loop and pull tight so knot is on opposite side of bead. You now have a bead with simple forehand knot on each side.

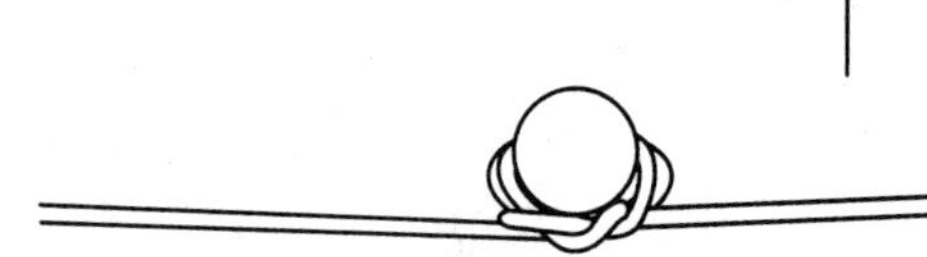

Diagram 113

D. Remove wire from vise and continue working it around bead by forcing end through openings between knots. **DO NOT COVER UP ONE SIDE OF BEAD.** It is your choice whether to use up all wire or not. Be sure to keep wire in a flowing motion around and in back of bead. Make sue each is tied down when your finish.

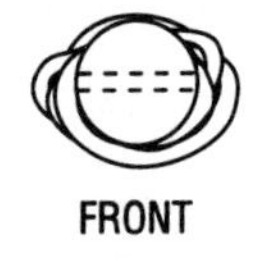

Diagram 114

E. Take piece of 20 gauge square wire and put 1/2" bend in one end. This will be the pin wire.

F. Force long end of wire under wires on back of stone. You may have to do a bit of prying with slender knife blade to get this wire through so other end hooks over wire in wrap around bead.

G. Make sure pin wire is **UNDER** at least two wires on back of bead.

Diagram 115

H. Wrap hook of pin wire two times around wires on back of bead, cut it and tuck end under one of wires making sure end is hidden so as not to snag.

I. Grasp pin wire with chain nose pliers on back of stone at point where it emerges form under bead. Hold firmly and slide pin vise on pin wire, tighten pin vise and twist all the way down shaft on pin wire, pulling back pin vise in 1/4" bites. Tug gently while twisting.

J. Cut off end of pin wire at sharp angle for beginning of point. *Diagram 116*

Diagram 116

K. File all the way around tip vigorously to make a good sharp point. Test it by putting it through several pieces of material. Slip clutch on end for completed stick pin.

L. An interesting variation of this system is to follow the same procedure, pages 81 through 83 without using a bead. Keep tying wire in knots. When completed, it can be left as is or pounded flat with plastic mallet. It makes a very striking stick pin.

Stickpin Variation (without bead)

#2 BEAD STICKPIN

Bead Stickpin

Materials: One 6mm drilled bead
One 6 1/2" length of 20 gauge wire square
One stick pin clutch

A. Put wire vertically in vise so approximately 1/8" sticks through top. File corners off and keep filing it evenly so wire will go into drilled beads.

B. Loosen vise and pull wire up 1/8" and repeat Step A. Repeat Step A until 1/4" of wire goes through bead.

C. Put wire through bead. Grasping short end protruding through bead with wide nose pliers, bend long end around bead as shown in *Diagram 117.*

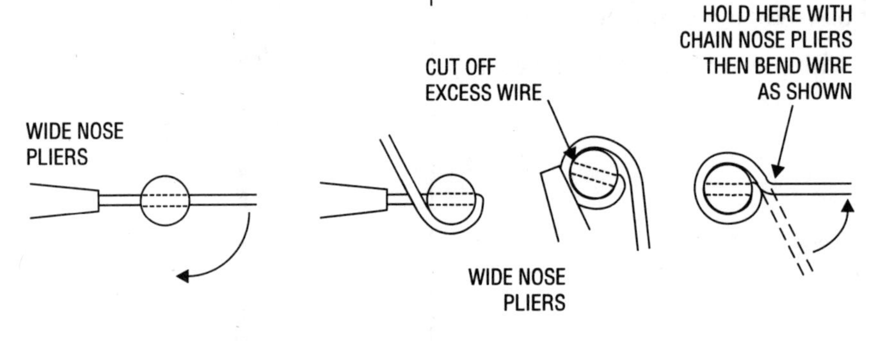

Diagram 117

D. Repeat Steps J and K as you did with Bird Nest Bead on page 83.

E. Finished product should look like *Diagram 118.*

F. It is important to note all stick pin shafts should be twisted. This adds strength to shaft. Also, when putting on stick pin, grip shaft firmly between thumb and forefinger as close to point as possible and force it through material. This will insure least damage to shaft for a longer period of time.

Diagram 118

#1 SMALL SHARK'S TOOTH WITH A SINGLE WIRE

Materials: One slender shark's tooth 1" or less
One 6" length of 21 gauge round wire

A. Put wire vertically on the back of the tooth. Leave about 1/2" to 1" of wire sticking below point of tooth. Bend other end as shown around left prong of tooth. *Diagram 119*

B. Continue wrapping wire around right prong of tooth as shown in *Diagram 120*

C. Take end of wire you are bending and slip it through vortex between right and left prong of tooth and under wires that are there, pull it tight.

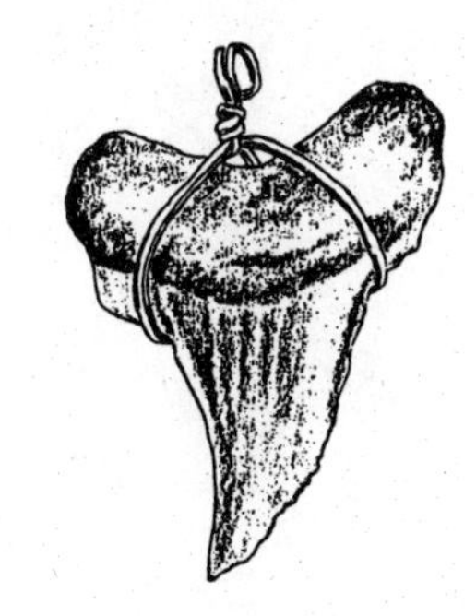

Single Wire Shark's Tooth

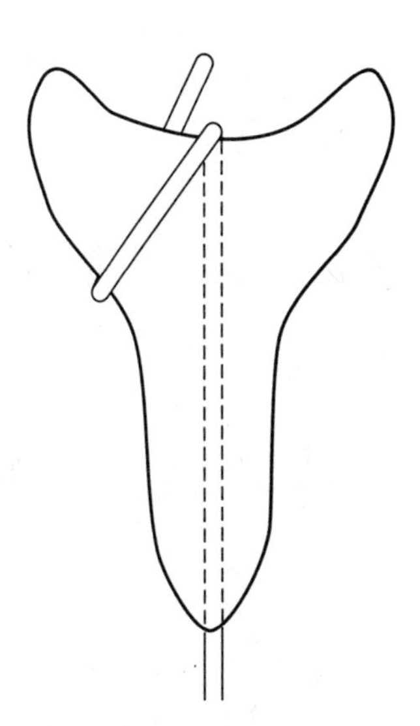

Diagram 119

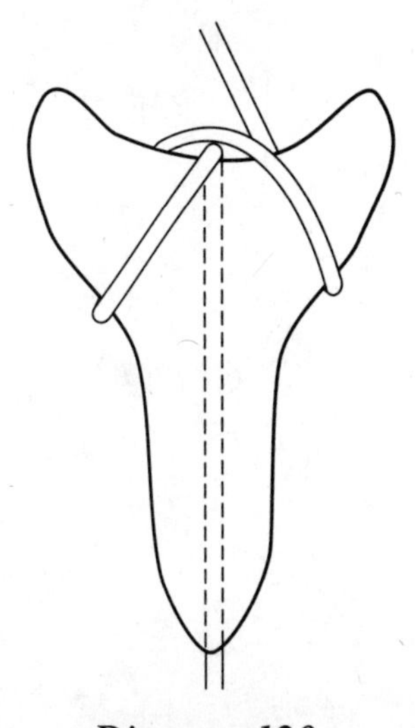

Diagram 120

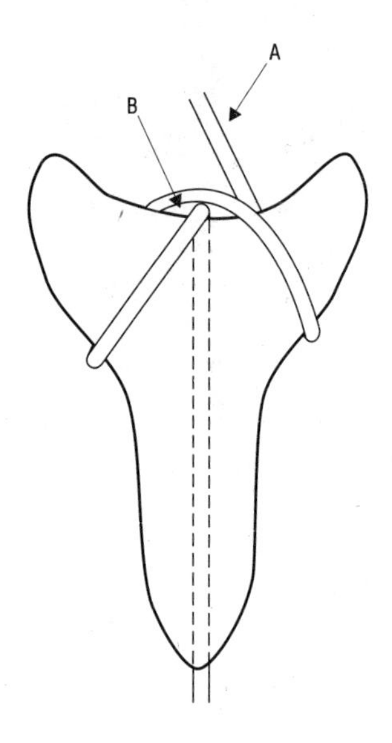

Diagram 121

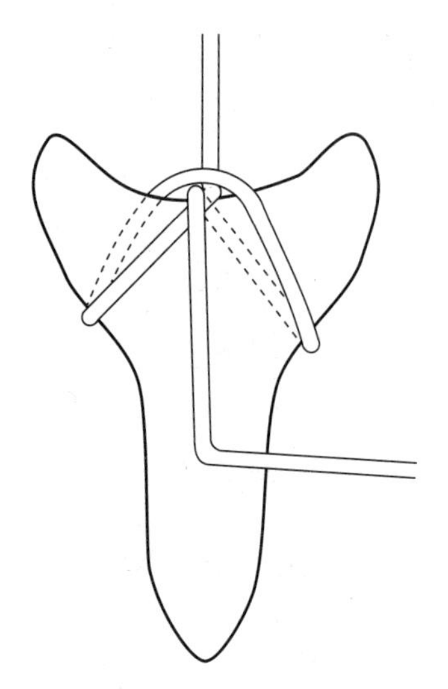

Diagram 122

D. Put wire A through space B and pull it tight. You may want to put it through again for added stability.

E. Turn tooth over and proceed as shown. *Diagram 122*

F. Bend wire around tooth just above point and tuck it under back as indicated. You may want to wrap it around back wire one and a half times. Cut if off and tuck under.

G. Finish off top as shown. Roll top wire around large part of needle nose until it is just above left and right prongs of tooth. Finish off clasp as shown. *Diagram 125*

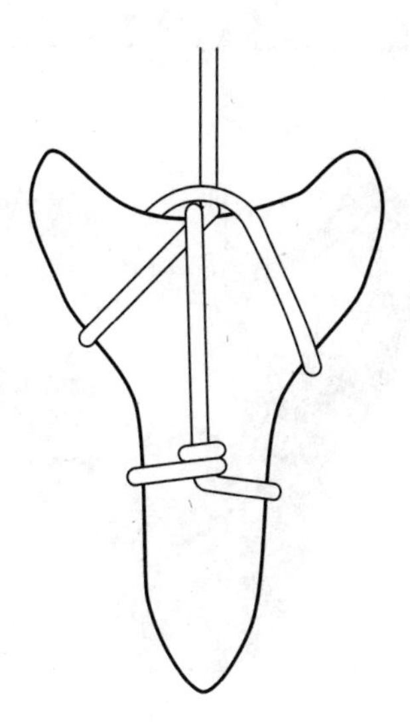

Diagram 123

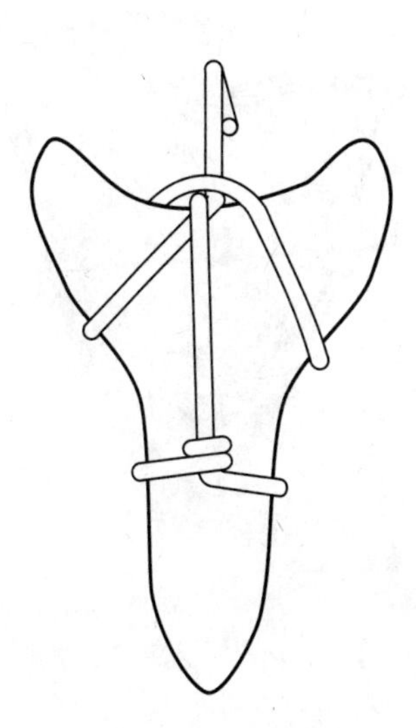

Diagram 124

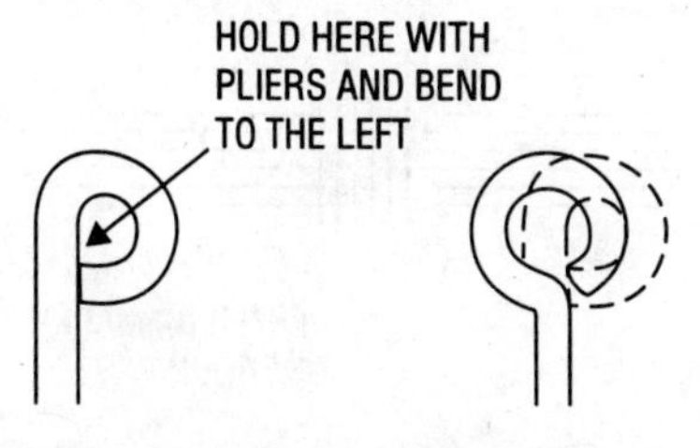

Diagram 125

#2 LARGE SHARK'S TOOTH (3" - 5")

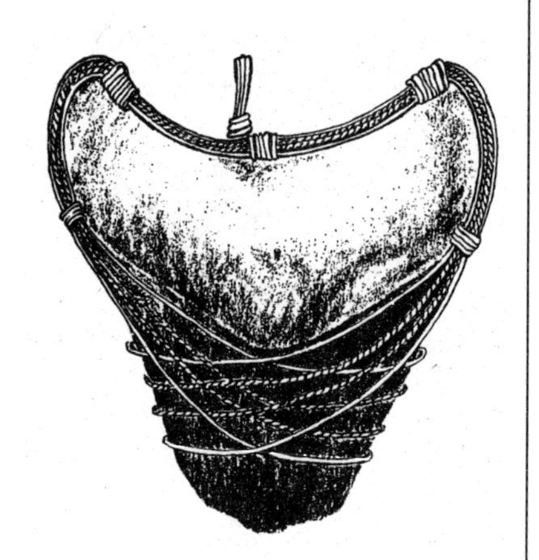

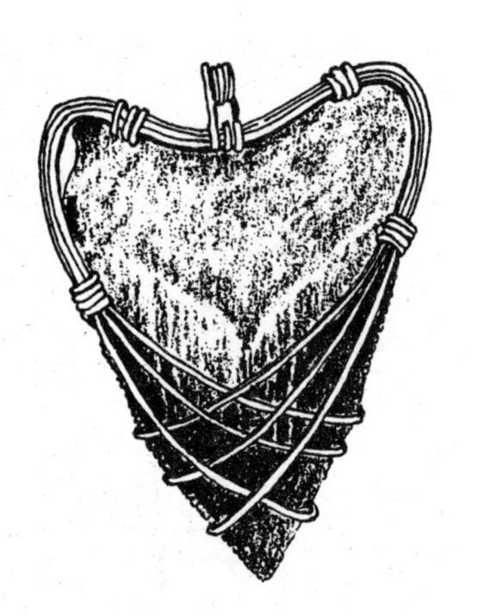

Large Sharks' Teeth

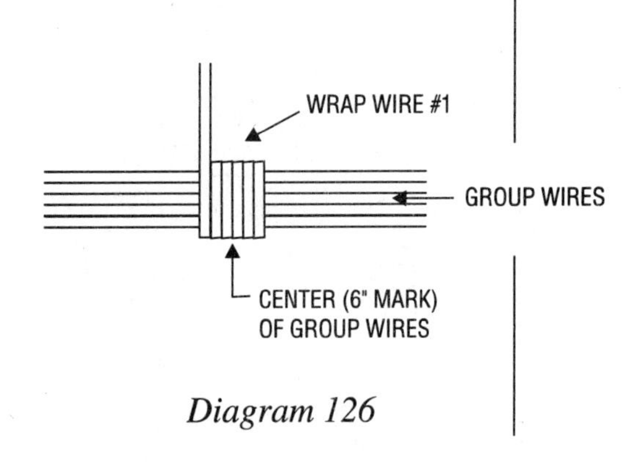

Diagram 126

Materials: One very large shark's tooth in good shape and condition.
Five wires 12" long, 20 gauge square.
One wire 5" long, 20 gauge square (wrap wire #1); bend over this wire 1/2" on one end.
Four wires 3" long, 20 gauge square (wrap wires #2,3,4,5); bend these over 1/2" on one end.

A. Tape five 12" wires together so they are flat and even.

B. At center of these 12" wires, attach wrap wire 1. Wrap it around five times, It must be in center as shown. *Diagram 126*

WHEN WRAPPING A TOOTH THIS SIZE, KEEP IN MIND:

1. An odd number of wires is more appealing to the eye.

2. For a more striking design, twist three center wires.

3. Make sure all wrap wires are put on as indicated.

4. Wrap wires should be wrapped around group wires so it can be bent over wrap and tooth and tied to anchor wire on back.

5. Pay particular attention to diagrams about how to put wrap wires on.

   Diagram 127 is a life-size front view of finished tooth. Following this large diagram are three smaller ones that are related to putting wrap wires on properly.

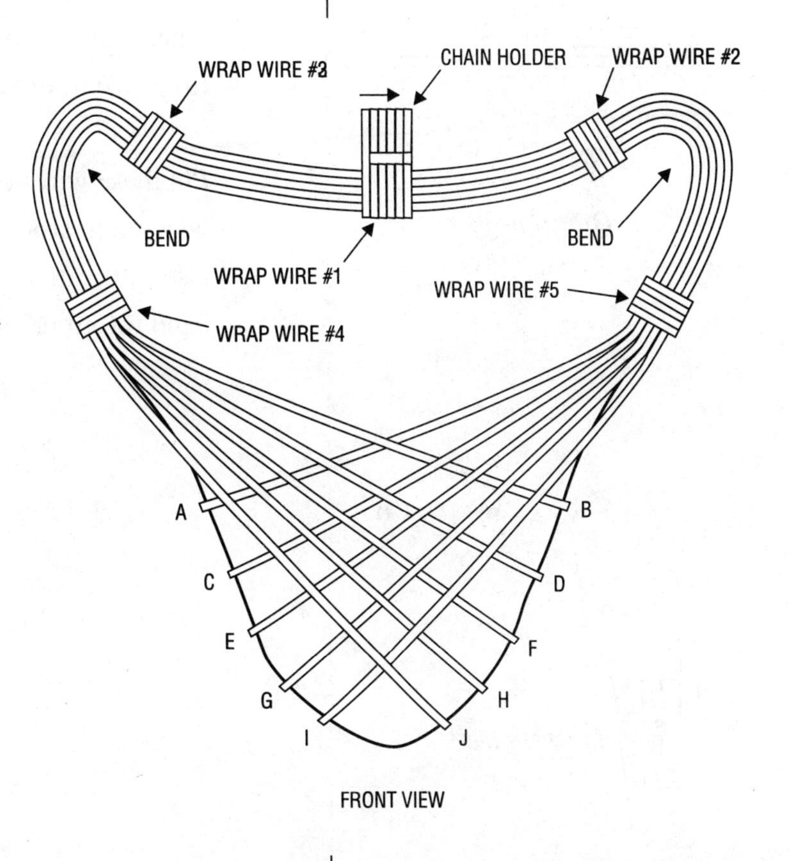

Diagram 127

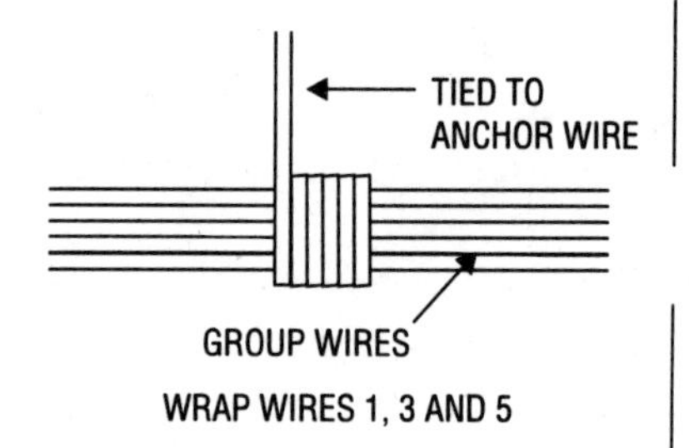

Diagram 128

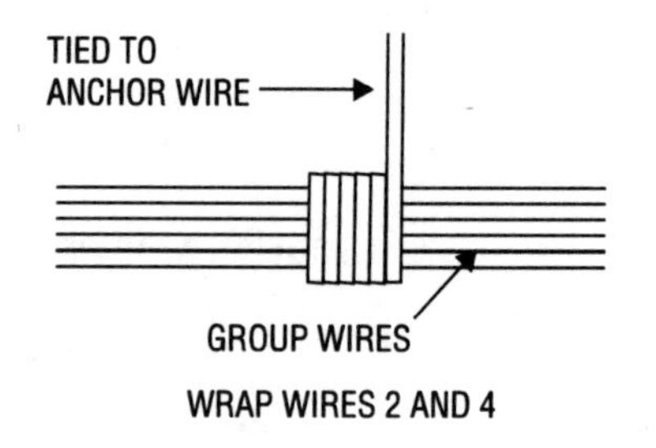

Diagram 129

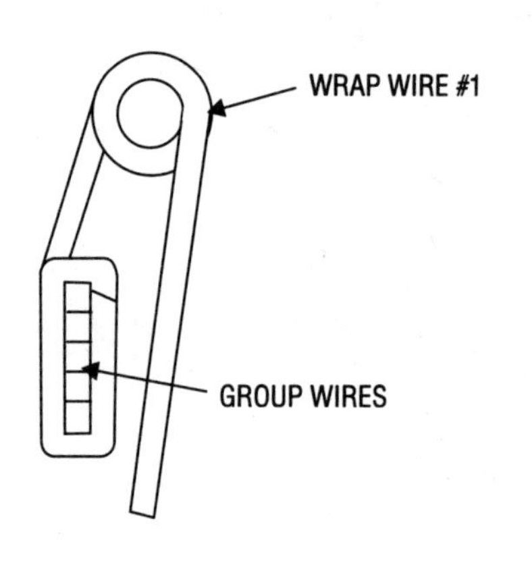

Diagram 130

C. Diagrams 128 & 129 show wrap wires.

D. *Diagram 130* shows wrap wire 1, side view, greatly enlarged.

Make as many loops here with needle nose pliers as are around group wires. It is important to make them to right side. Offset left-sided wrap around group wires. (see front view diagram.) This is to be tied to the center of anchor wire on back of tooth.

E. Size of tooth will determine where to place wrap wires 2 and 3. Common sense should dictate they be of equal distance from wrap wire 1 and still be close (or far) enough (to or from) to keep group wires flat while bending them.

F. Put these wires on group wires before you attempt to bend them around tooth. **THIS IS IMPERATIVE.** It is also imperative not to put on wrap wire 4 and 5 until the bend (of group wires) is complete.

G. Use wide nose pliers to help you make the bend. Hold group wires by clamping down firmly on wrap wire 2 which is wrapped around group wires. Hold with pliers and bend and shape slowly - **VERY SLOWLY**. Do not try to bend wires one at a time. It will detract from the design. *Diagram 131*

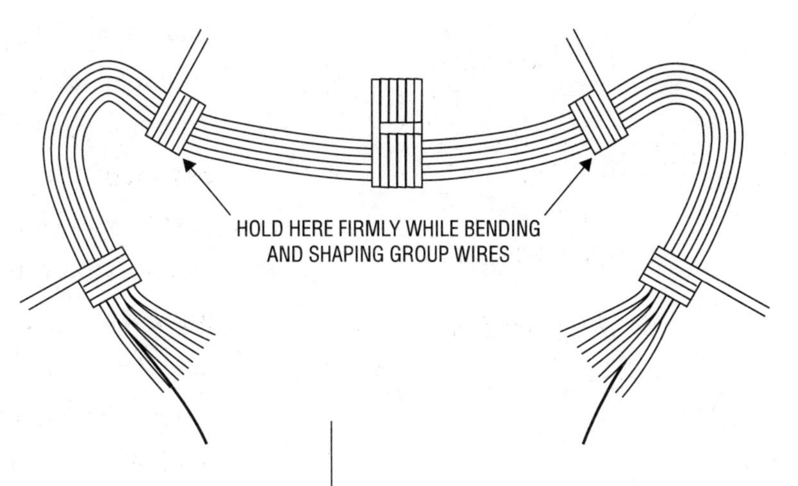

Diagram 131

H. Once again, common sense should dictate location of wrap wires 4 and 5. Just be sure they are even with each other and high enough on group wires to get a good "net" effect.

I. *Diagram 132* is a side view of the chain holder as it should be fastened on front and back of tooth. The chain holder is simply an extension of wrap wire 1 tied to anchor wire on back after several loops are made in it.

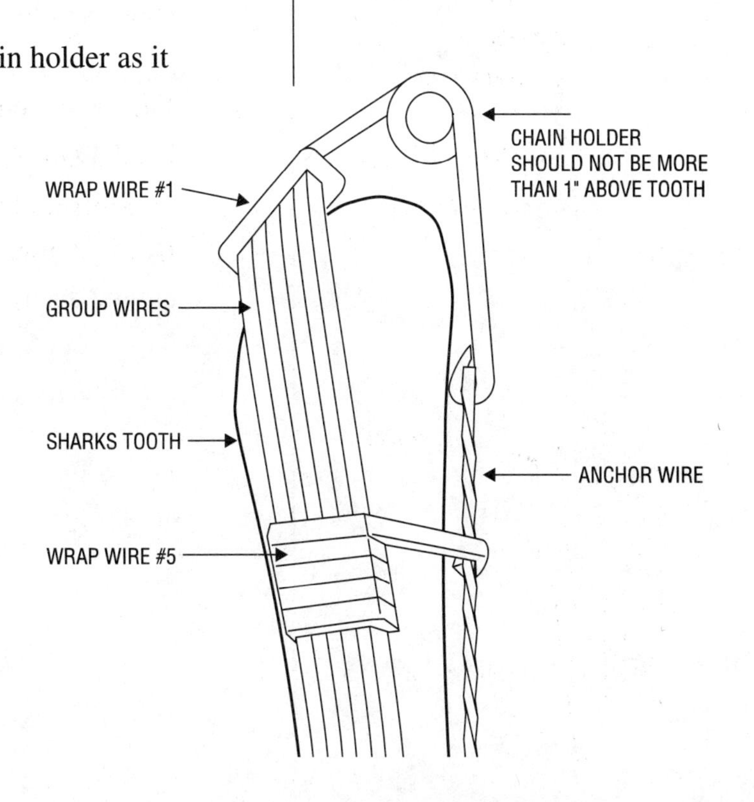

Diagram 132

J. It is imperative anchor wire be twisted with pin vise to give it added strength.

K. Join ends of anchor wire after bending it in triangular shape by looping them around each other and wrapping ends around wire as shown. **FLATTEN LOOPS WITH PLIERS.**

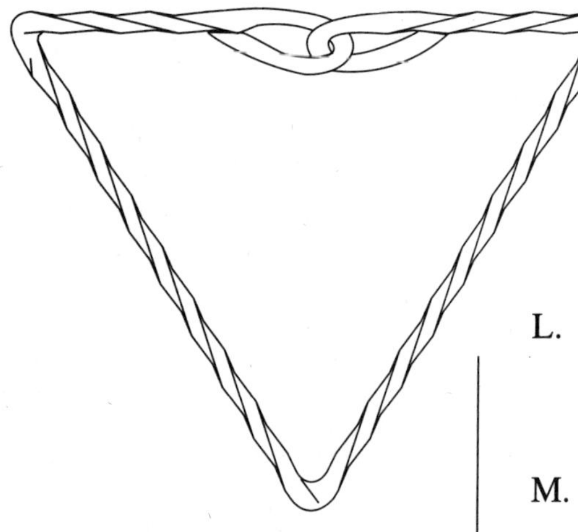

Diagram 133

L. Tape anchor wire to back of tooth. Keep it near top and in center of tooth.

M. Tie down wrap wire 1 (temporarily) to anchor wire — **DO NOT** cut off all of excess yet.

N. Bend wrap wires 4 and 5 around back of tooth and loop it around anchor wire once (temporarily tie down.) **DO NOT** cut off excess yet. Make them tight enough to hold group wires down along each side of tooth.

O. Now do likewise with group wires A, then B.

P. Now do same with wrap wires 2, then 3.

Q. Now do same with group wires C through J in alphabetical order. *(See front view diagram on page 89)* **DO NOT LET ANCHOR WIRE SLIP DOWN TOWARD BOTTOM OF TOOTH**. Keep taking up slack in wrap wires 1, 2, and 3 if necessary.

R. As each wire is tied to anchor wire, make sure they are on equal distance apart on front of tooth.

S. Tighten all wires by looping them one and a half times around anchor wire. Cut off excess and tuck under any loose ends. Wrap is now complete.

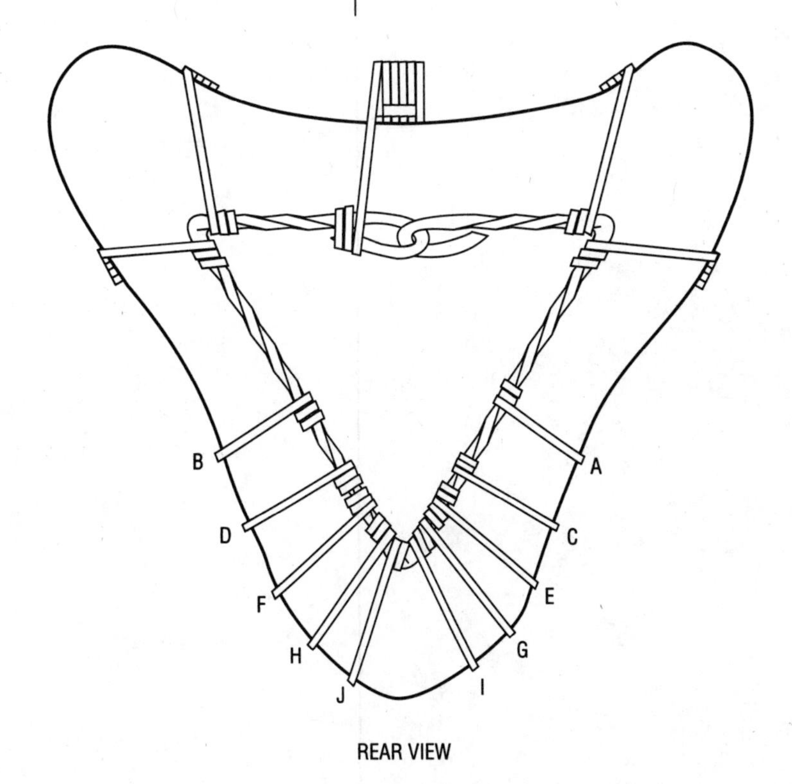

Diagram 134

#1 THE SPIDER BODY

Tiger Eye, Malachite, Paua Shell, or Turquoise make the best looking spiders. For the first attempt you may want to use brass practice wire and cabochons with a high bevel. (High dome cabs are more difficult.)

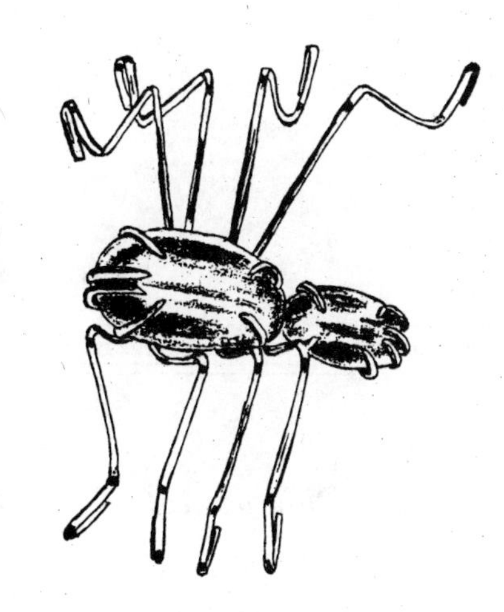

Spider

Materials: All wires are 20 gauge, square
Nine wires, 8" long optional (large) 6" for smaller
Two wires 3" long (wrap wires, bend over one end of each 1/2")
One 18mm x 25mm cabochon (body of spider)
One 10mm x 14mm cabochon (head of spider)
One Kitchen Knife

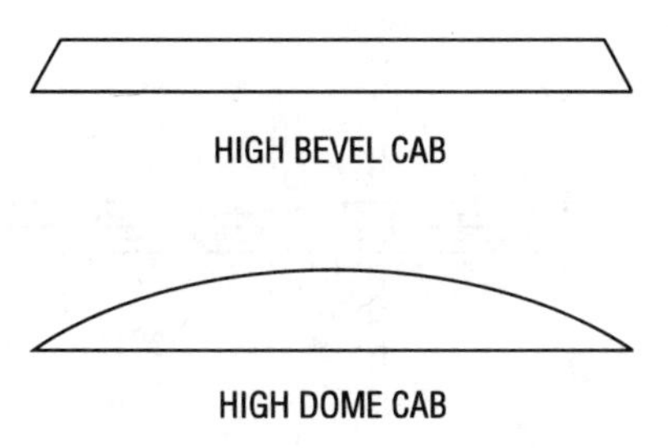

A. Arrange all of 8" wires together as shown. *Diagram 135*

B. Using one of 3" wrap wires, wrap it around group of nine wires four times as shown. Please note where 4" line is marked.

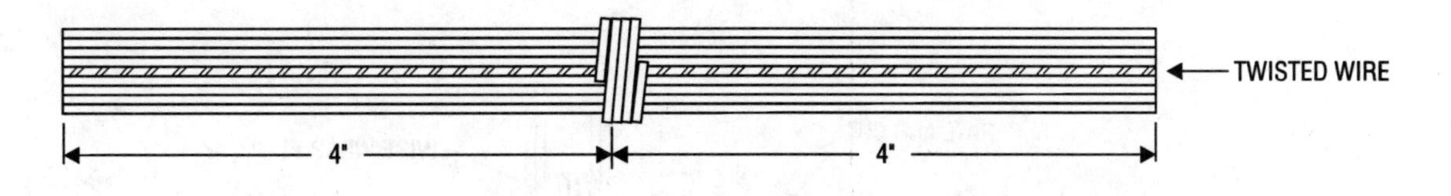

Diagram 135

NOTE: LARGE SPIDER IS SHOWN IN ALL DIAGRAMS.

C. Bend two outside group wires on both sides as shown. Bend them one at a time, 90 degrees so they are perpendicular to remaining group wires. *Diagram 136*

D. Slide back leg wires so they are 2-1/4" from one end, as shown. (Distances between wrap wires are approximate. They can vary without affecting the design.) *Diagram 137*

E. Now wrap remaining five wires with other wrap wire as shown (2 1/2" from the first wrap - see *Diagram 138*).

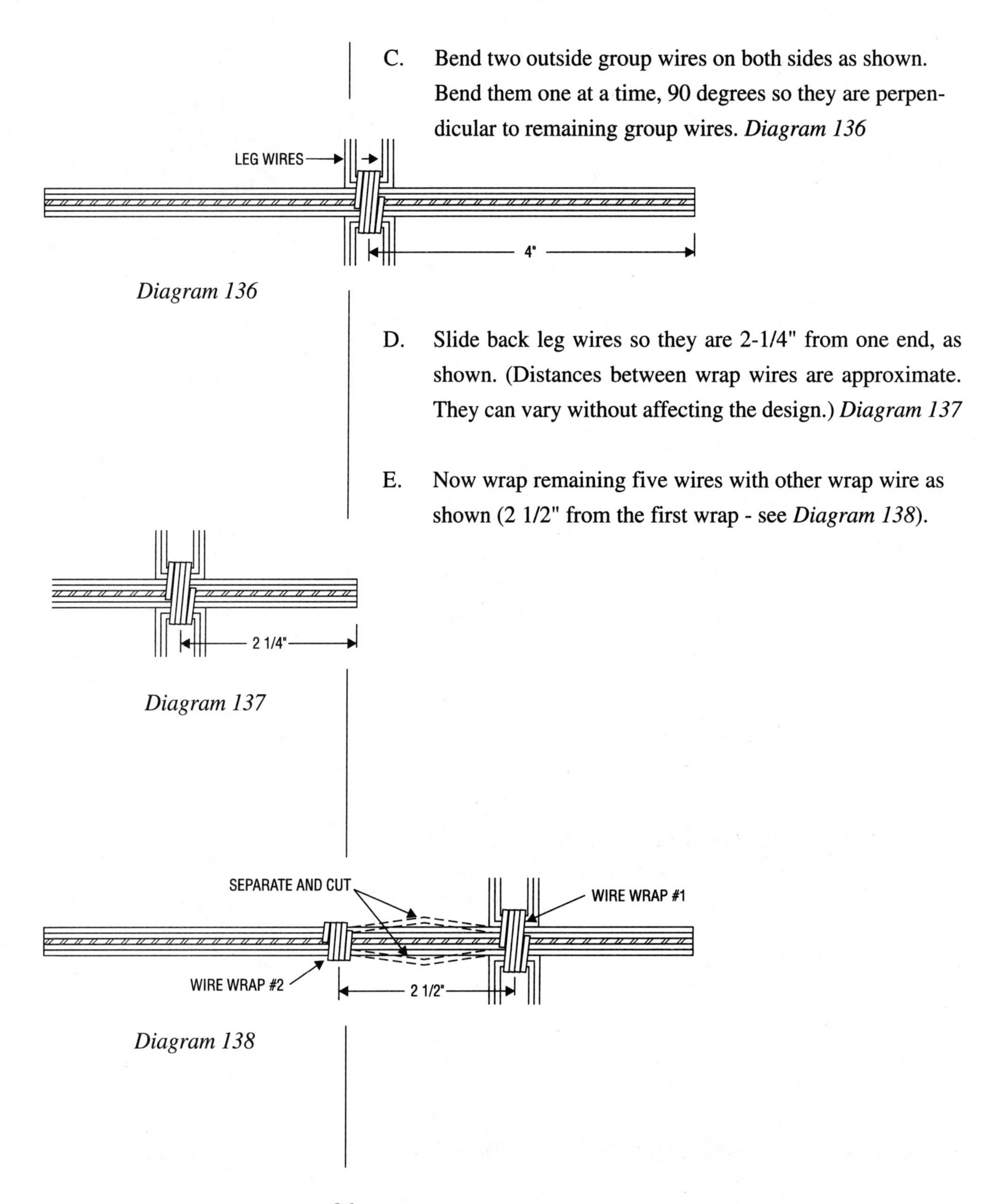

Diagram 136

Diagram 137

Diagram 138

F. Separate two outside wires and cut them halfway between wrap wires and spread them as shown. *Diagram 139*

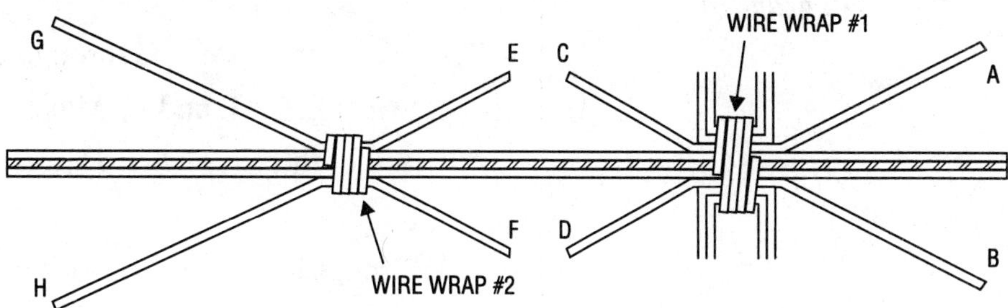

G. Wires should look like the above diagram. Make sure ends of wrap wires are all on same side.

H. Place entire assembly on flat surface. Make sure ends of wrap wires are facing up. Place an 18mm x 25mm cabochon directly on top of wrap wire 1.

For an effective spider, make sure wrap wire is to left of center of cabochon as in *Diagram 140*.

I. While holding cabochon in place, bend wires A, B, C, and D across top of stone as shown. *Diagram 141*

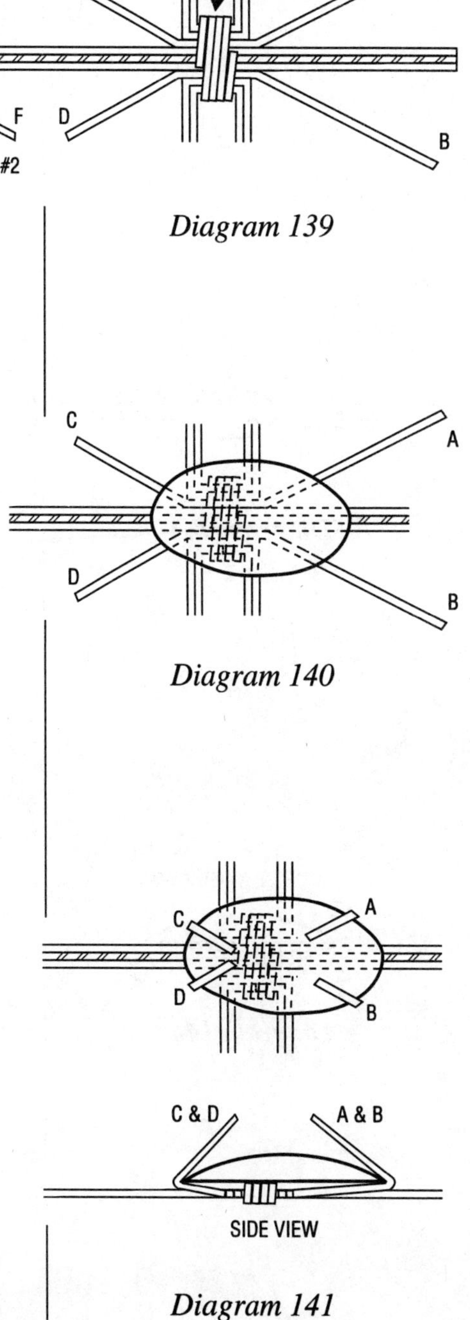

Diagram 139

Diagram 140

Diagram 141

NOTE: LARGE SPIDER IS SHOWN IN ALL DIAGRAMS.

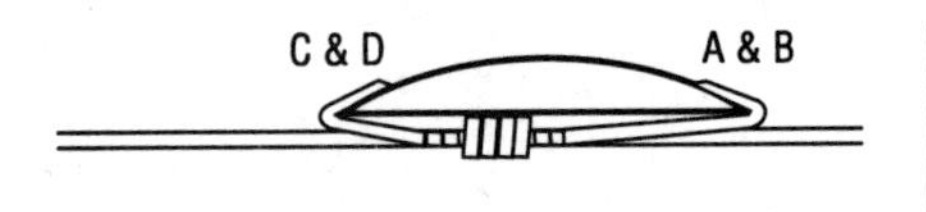

Diagram 142

J. Cut off wires A, B, C, and D as indicated. Be sure actual cut is parallel to the group wire on the flat surface.

K. Now repeat steps G through I using smaller cabochon and wires E, F, G, and H. Make sure cabochon is centered on top of the wrap wire. *Diagram 143*

L. Prongs holding cabochons in place can be worked tight by gently squeezing them, as shown, with the wide nose pliers. *Diagram 144*

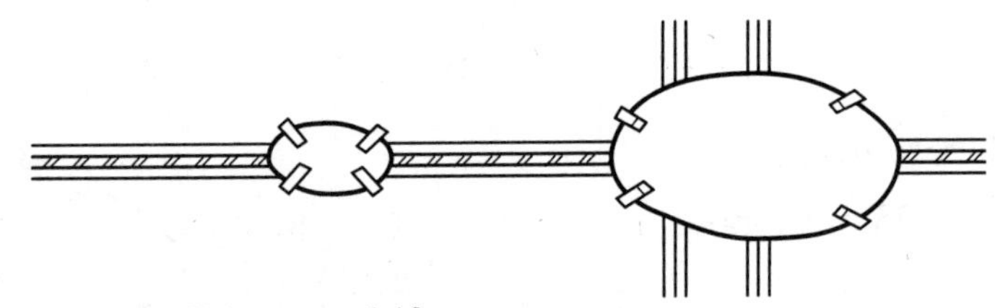

Diagram 143

Diagram 144

M. Now, with wide nose pliers, pull the two mounted cabochons (assembly) together. Grasp larger cabochon in left hand, thumb on top of cabochon and forefinger underneath and over wrap wire 1. With right hand, pull small cabochon assembly back toward large assembly. *Diagram 145*

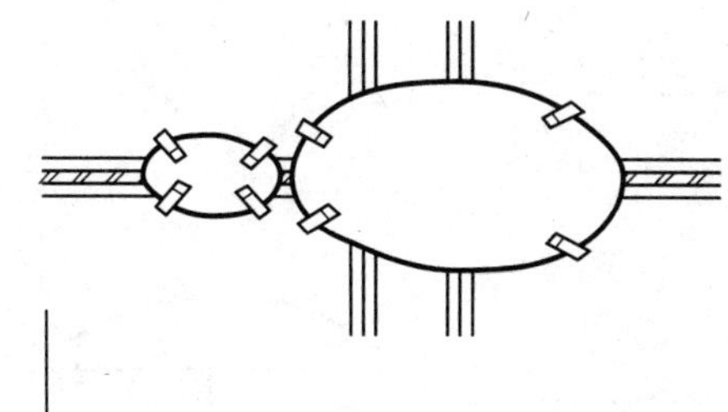

Diagram 145

N. Now twist the long center wire.

O. Bend up last two front group wires (one on either side of center wire) as shown: **DO NOT** bend up center twisted wire.

P. Cut off two remaining group wires same as other prong wires in Step J.

Q. Make sure two cabochons are snug up against each other (end to end), then bend remaining two group wires in rear. Simply repeat step O. **DO NOT** bend up twisted wire. Spider should now look like *Diagram 148.*

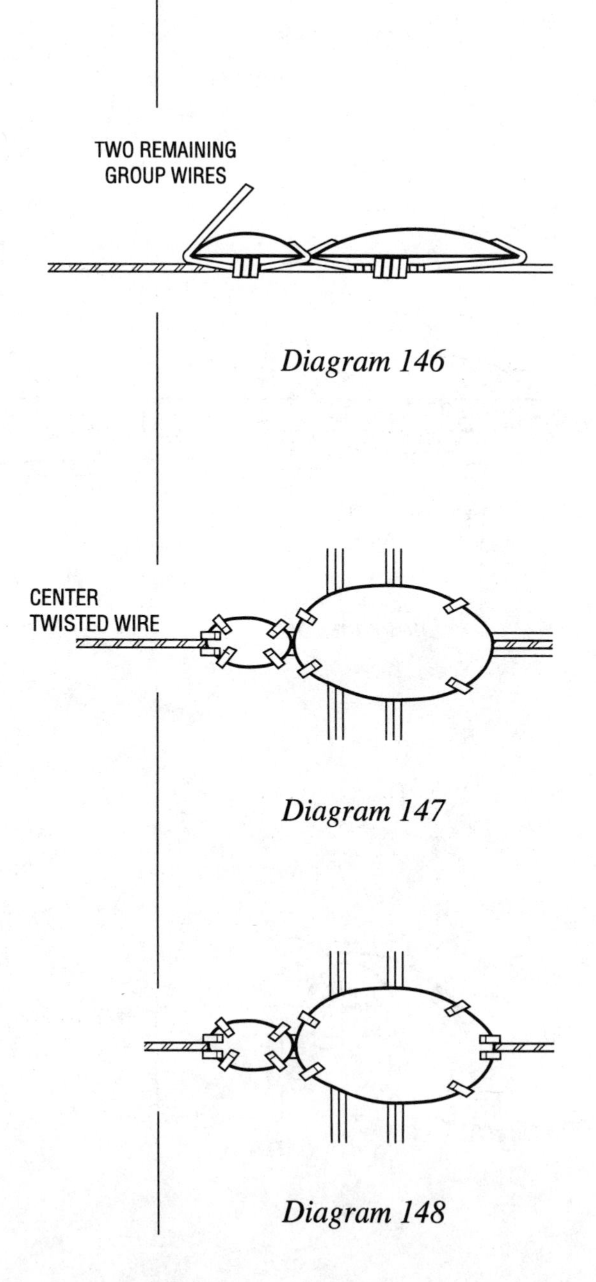

Diagram 146

Diagram 147

Diagram 148

Q. Bend down twisted wire at rear of spider as shown, then loop it one complete turn around midway point of one of jaws of needle nose pliers. *Diagram 149*

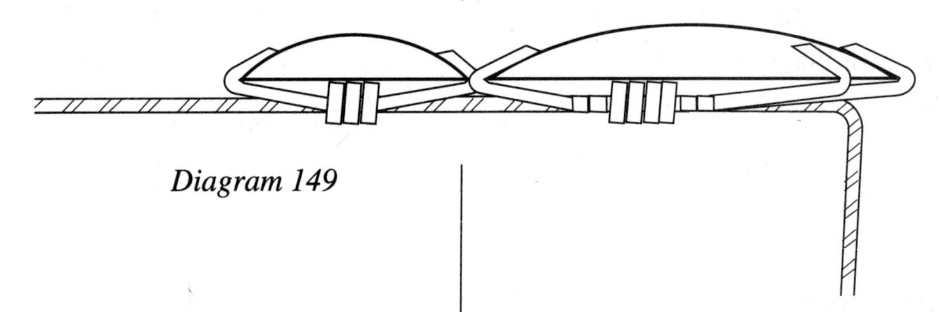

Diagram 149

R. Make loop as close to spider as possible. You may have to bend it sideways to make a complete loop. When loop is completed, bend it back so it is perpendicular to bottom of spider. *Diagram 150*

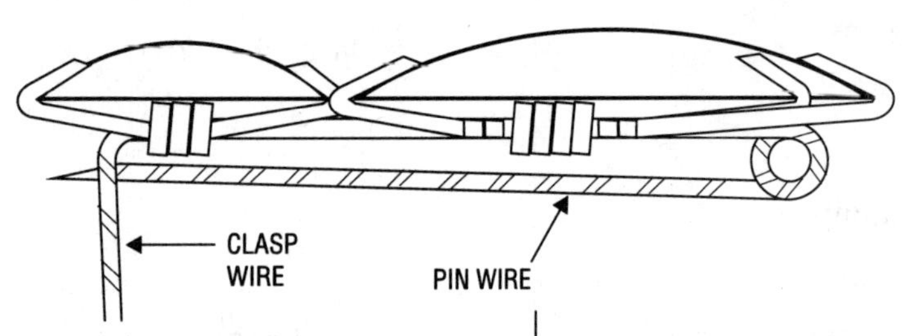

Diagram 150

S. Bend down other end of twisted wire as shown in *Diagram 150.*

T. Grasp the clasp wire with needle nose pliers 5/16" below spider (with front end of spider looking at jaws of pliers). Bend clasp wire back up in opposite direction, then cut it off and bend again as shown. *Diagram 151*

The spider body is now complete.

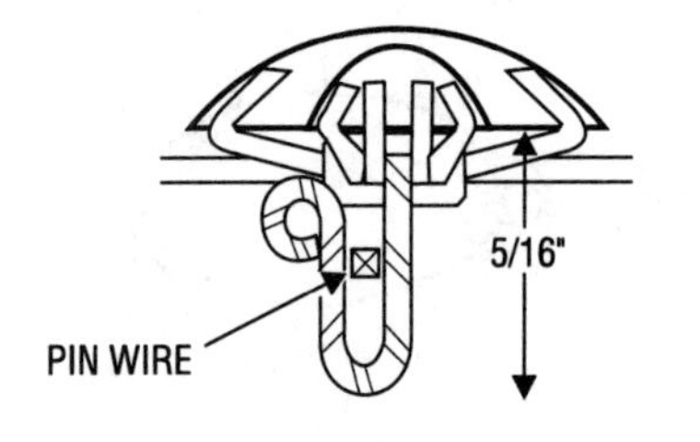

Diagram 151

#2 SPIDER LEGS

A. **(For Large Spiders)** Hold body of spider firmly with thumb and forefinger of left hand and bend up leg wires (approximately) 60 degrees. Bend two at a time as shown (with thumb and forefinger of right hand). *Diagram 152*

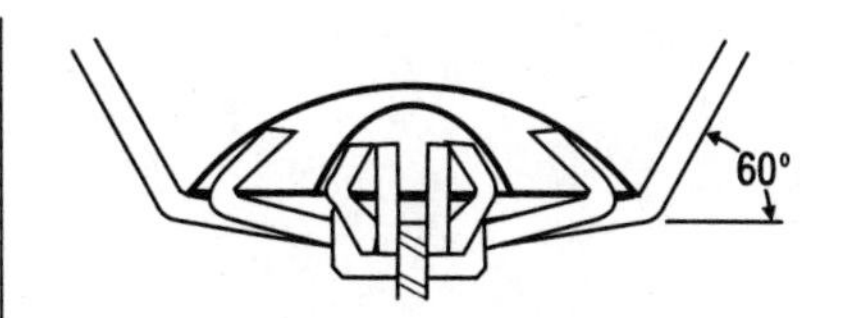

Diagram 152

(For Small Spiders) Adjust accordingly. Make sure the third bend makes spider leg come down below spider pin.

B. Now bend four pair of legs (using wide nose or needle nose as needed). *Diagram 153*

C. It is imperative to be very careful with leg wires. Do not try to straighten them out once they are bent. If any adjustment is required, use point X for required adjustments and be very gentle.

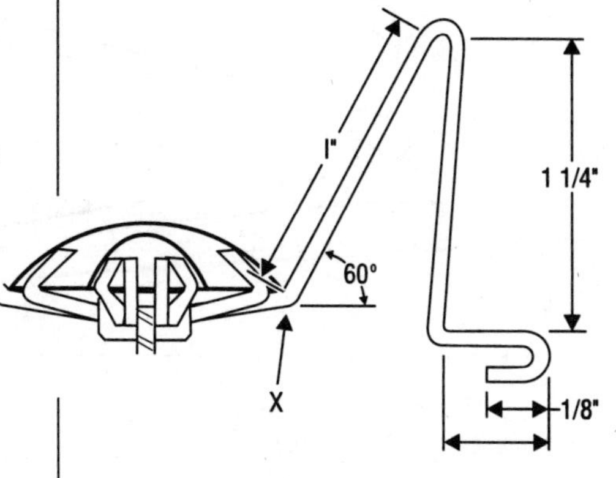

Diagram 153

D. Using kitchen knife, pry apart four pairs of legs so they are an equal distance apart for eight legged spider. File pin wire down to fine point. When pinning this spider on cloth, grasp pin wire in back of point and force it through the material. Spider is very effective when worn in front of the left shoulder high up on the chest.

NOTE: LARGE SPIDER IS SHOWN IN ALL DIAGRAMS.

#3 SPIDER WEB

A. Find a three pronged branch similar to *Diagram 154.* These dimensions are very flexible. A good branch of this general shape will do. The three pronged branch is ideal to set on a T.V. or a rec-room shelf. For a web to hang on a wall, a two prong branch will work.

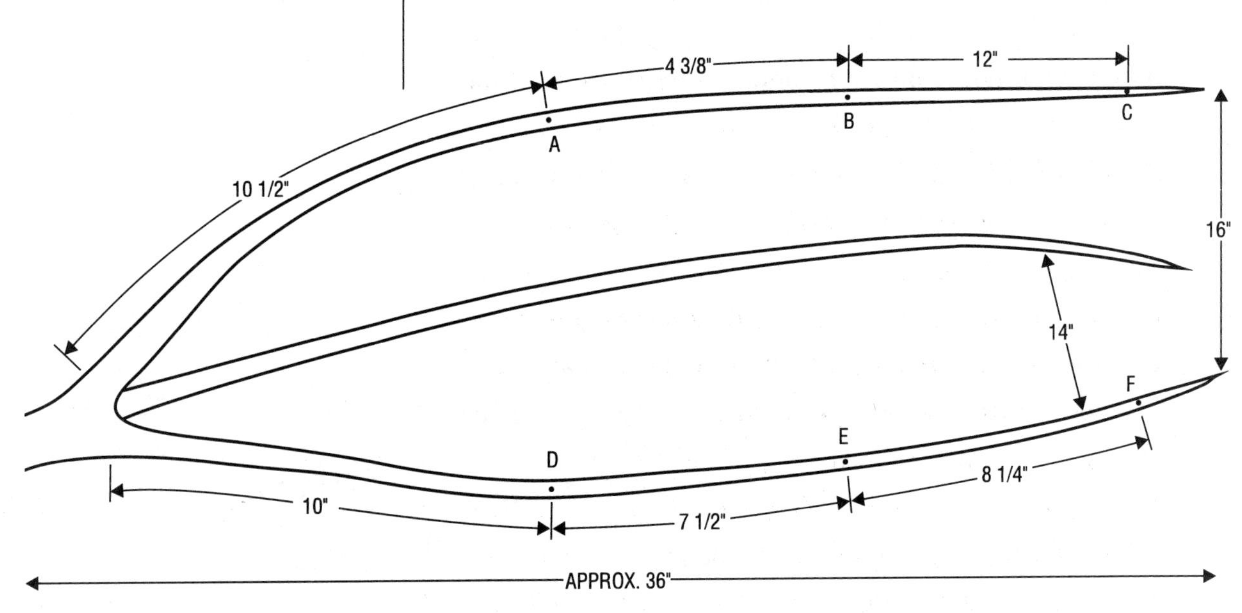

Diagram 154

B. Using a 1/16" drill bit (electric drill), drill holes at points A, B, C, D, E, and F. The placing of these holes is arbitrary. They will be used for anchor wires; I only use three anchor wires — any number of anchor wires can be used. Remember, the placement and number of these anchor wires determine the pattern of the web.

C. In making all webs, anchor wires **MUST BE TWISTED**. All dimensions given here are for this size branch only and for only three anchor wires. It is also strongly advised that brass wire be used if this is your first attempt at making a web.

D. The dimensions of the anchor wires are as follows and refers to letters in the diagram:

1. A - F is 24" length, including plenty of surplus.
2. C - D is 24" length, including plenty of surplus.
3. B - E is 15" length, including plenty of surplus.

Twist wires, one at a time by putting one end of wire in small jewelers's bench vise. Put other end of wire through pin vise. Slide pin vise down wire until it is about 1/2" from end in bench vise. Tighten pin vise so it grips wire with pin vise, then slide pin vise back 1/2" and twist again. Repeat this process until entire length of wire has been twisted. To prevent wire from being twisted in half (or broken) use chain nose pliers to hold wire (while it is still in bench vise) about 1/2" from pin vise. As the twisting progresses, move pliers back along twisted wire as pin vise is moved. It must be held firmly in order to keep rest of wire from turning as full length is twisted. **TWIST ALL ANCHOR WIRES IN THIS MANNER**. Some wirewrappers use an egg-beater drill to twist long wires.

E. Insert appropriate wire through their corresponding holes. **DO NOT CUT OFF SURPLUS YET**. Make sure there is at least 1" overlap through holes. With needle nose pliers, coil wires as shown. These wires can be tightened or loosened as temperature changes occur. *Diagram 155*

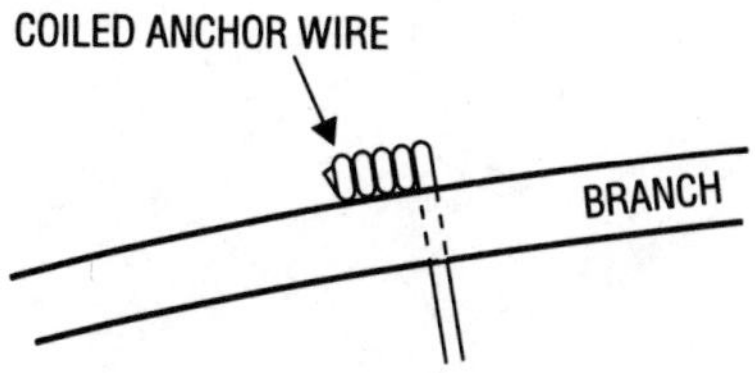

Diagram 155

F. When all anchor wires are in place, make sure they cross each other on **ONE** central vortex. To insure this central cross, tie them together temporarily with short piece of string (or wire).

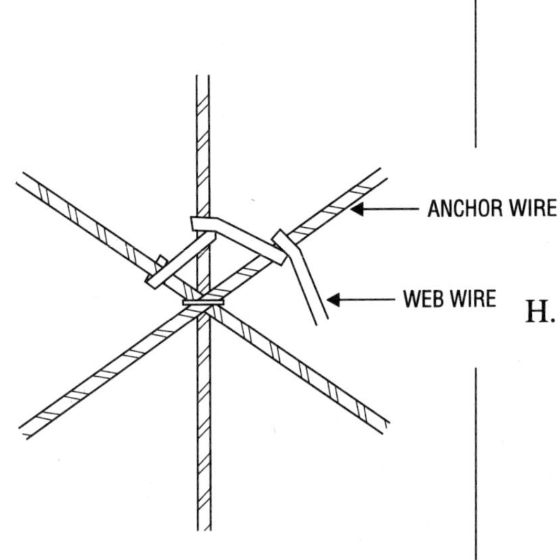

Diagram 156

G. Cut piece of square wire 3" long. (This is beginning of web.) Begin at the point where all wires cross. Bend end of 3" wire over 1/8". Hook it on one end of anchor wires, as close to the center as possible. Using wide nose pliers, squeeze it gently (**GENTLY!!** So it is secure. **CAUTION:** If squeezed too hard, it will cut the anchor wire, so be very careful.)

H. After end is secured, pass 3" wire over and completely around next anchor wire on right. (I always spin my webs in a clockwise motion.) Make sure each wrap around grips anchor wire securely as detailed in Step G. *Diagram 156*

I. When all of 3" wire is used up, make sure it ends gripping an anchor wire. (It is easier to work with a short piece of wire in center of web.) Cut, if necessary.

J. Now cut piece of wire 3' or 4' in length. Bend over one end of it 1/8" and with it, grip anchor wire at point where 3" wire ends (or is secure). Repeat Step H until entire web is spun. As you get further from the center, give the wires a draped look by pushing in gently with fingers mid-way between anchor wires. Web wires should always be flat, not turned. Also, they should be 1/2" - 3/4" apart. Keep wire flat at all times. *Diagram 157*

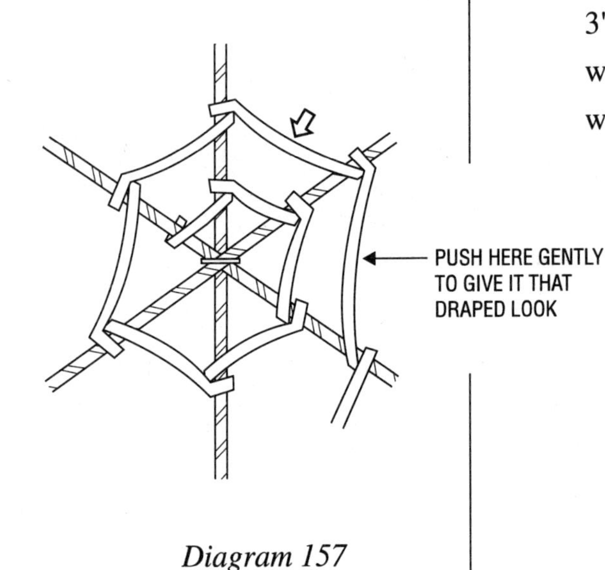

Diagram 157

K. This will give you some idea of what a finished web should look like. (Remember to remove the temporary piece of string put on in Step F.) *Diagram 158*

L. For an effective web, put a wire wrap spider in upper right corner. Near center, put a couple of oblong stones (1/8" x 1/2") with bird cage wraps. Tiger eye is most affective for a real looking spider in web. Oblong slivers of amazonite make very effective "bugs".

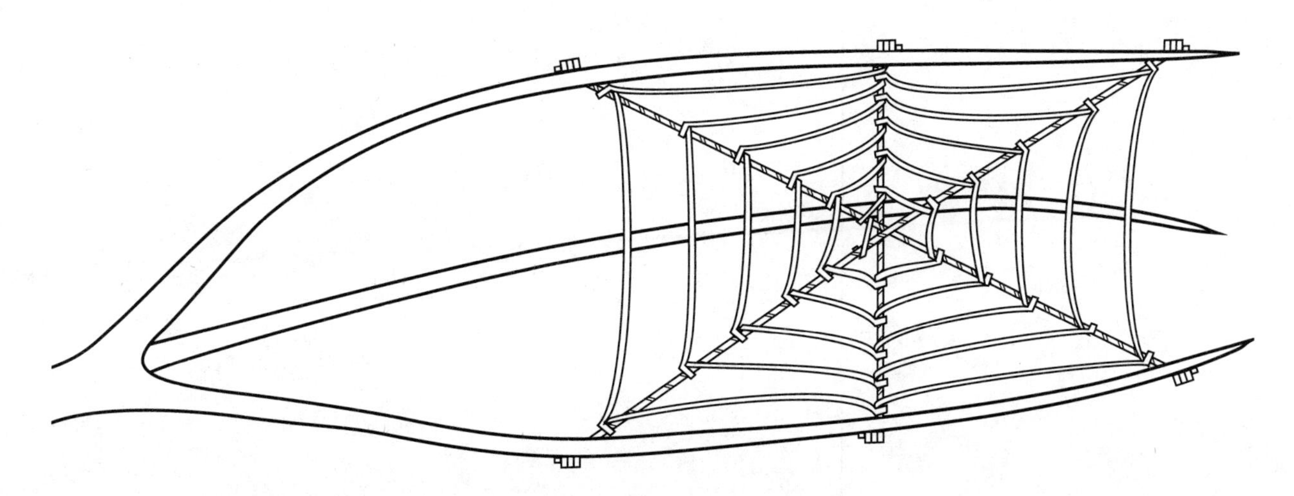

Diagram 158

CROSSES

A. Cut six pieces of wire 4" long, 21 gauge square.

B. Cut eight pieces of wire 2" long, 21 gauge square.

C. Bend over 1/4" one end of 2" wires.

D. Twist, with pin vise, two of the 4" wires.

E. Measure 1-1/2" of other two 4" wires and mark, then bend over 90 degrees as shown. **DO NOT BEND TWISTED WIRES.** *Diagram 159*

F. Using two of the bent (90 degree) wires and one of twisted 4" wires, put them together and wrap them with one of the 2" wrap wires as shown. Make sure wrap wire is as close to 90 degree bend as possible. *Diagram 160*

Also make sure wires are flat and remain flat as they are being wrapped.

Cross

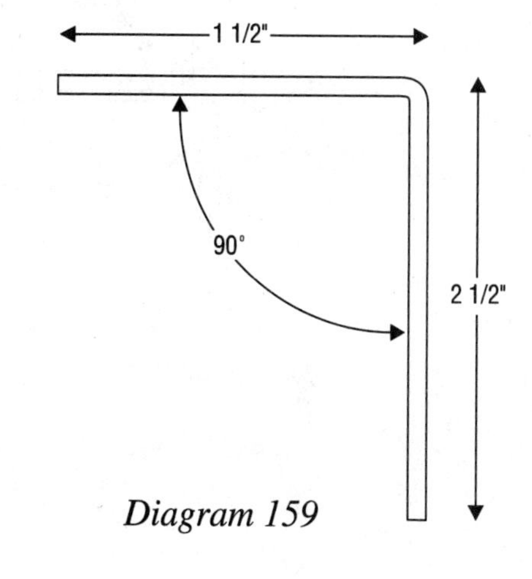

Diagram 159

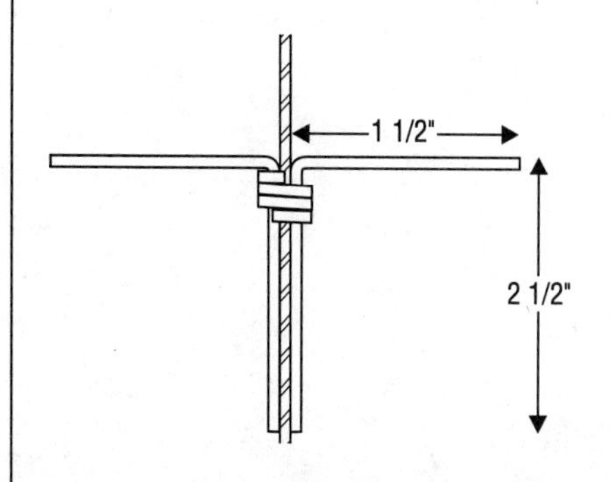

Diagram 160

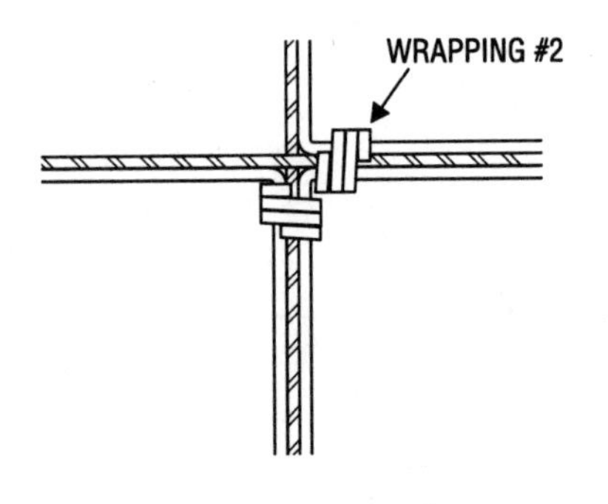

Diagram 161

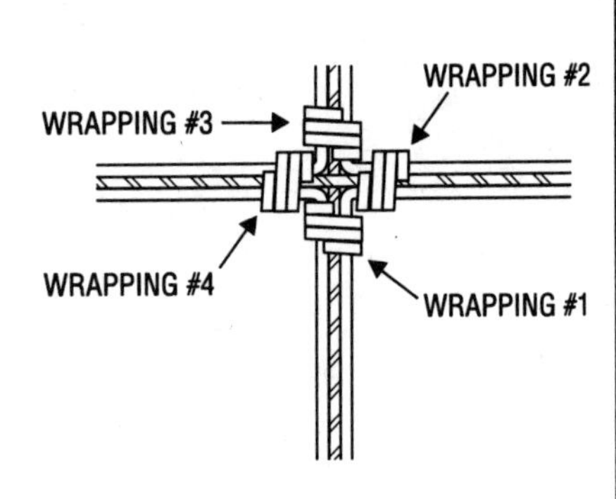

Diagram 162

G. Put other twisted wire perpendicular to first one; then, beside it, put another bent 4" wire parallel to it with short end pointing in same direction as first twisted wire. Wrap it with second wrap wire as shown. *Diagrams 161 & 162.*

H. Repeat Step F for upper left portion of cross and wrap wire 4. *Diagram 163*

IT IS IMPORTANT TO MAKE SURE ALL ENDS OF WRAP WIRES ARE ALL ON SAME SIDE.

I. Other four wrap wires will be put on outer extremities of the cross arms. Where they go will be determined by you choice of design. Suggested distance can be about 1/2" from other end of wires.

J. After wrap wires are put on outer extremities of cross, cut them off evenly and spread them. Suggestions for completion can be found below. The center wire at top of the cross can be made into a loop (for a chain).

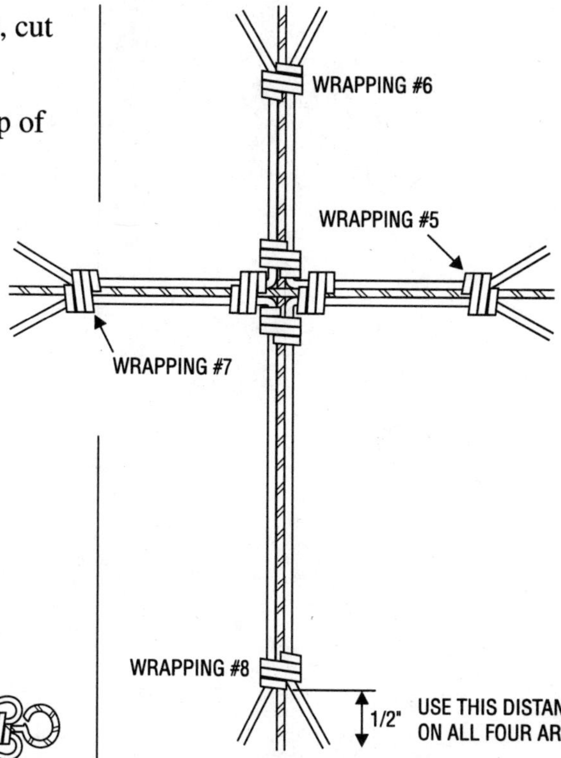

Diagram 163

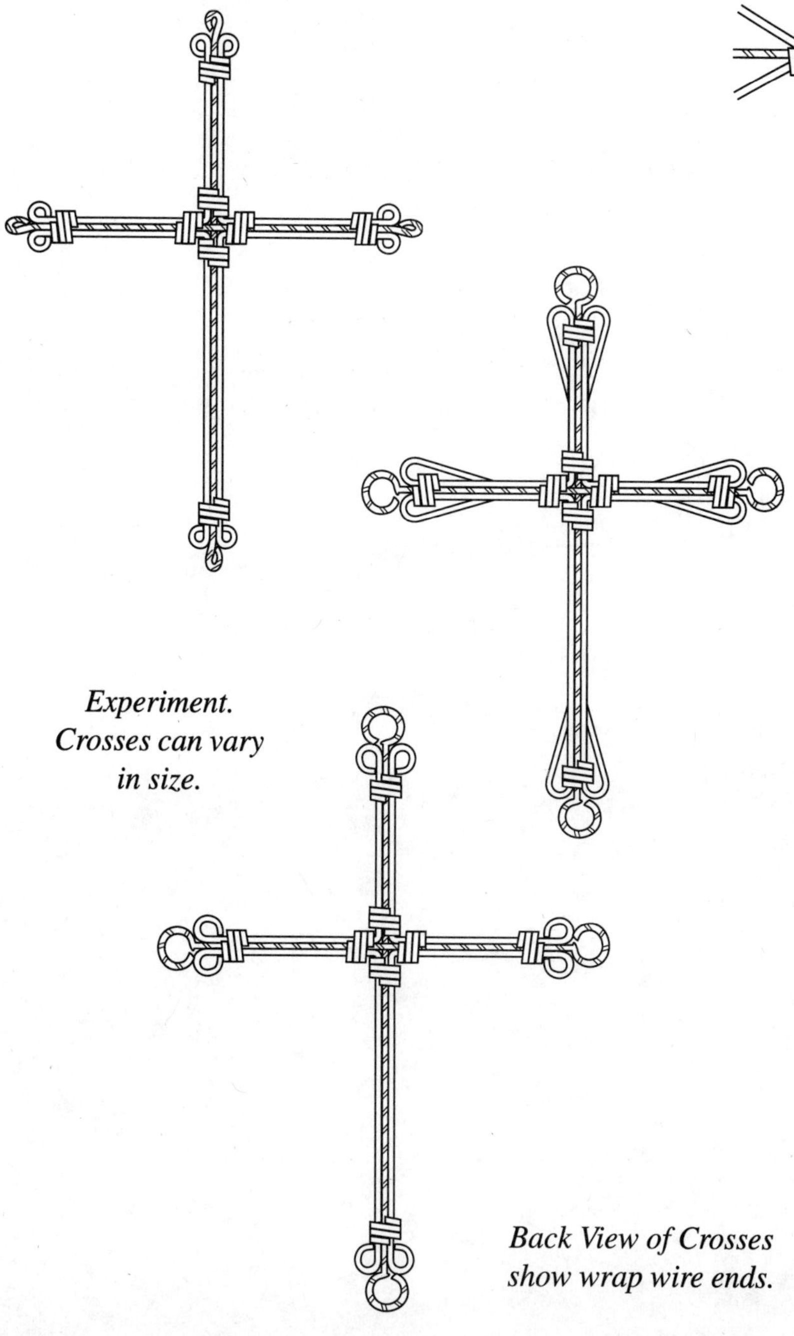

Experiment. Crosses can vary in size.

Back View of Crosses show wrap wire ends.

Chapter 11 — Epilogue

As a final note, I would like to leave you with a few thoughts that I'm sure many wirewrappers have had.

First of all, there are infinite variations of what has been presented in these pages. When a mistake is made or a wire breaks, don't be discouraged - continue on - use your imagination. It will lead to many, many new ideas, some of which may just be worth while. When a new idea comes along, develop it to its fullest potential.

There are three systems that have been purposely omitted from this book. Those systems are: chains, name pins, and tiffany mounts. Wire chains can be made easily, but they do consume a lot of wire. The cost factor, in my opinion, does not justify making them. There are already many books on the market about how to make name pins. They are fun and easy to do and nothing can be added to change the system significantly. Tiffany mounts are beautiful, but the degree of difficulty in making these rings does not justify (in my opinion) the end product.

In the event you have any problems with any system in this book, do not hesitate to drop a card in the mail. I can be reached at the following address:

E.E. Sinclair
P.O. Box 2011
Manassas, VA 22110

During my years as a wirewrapper, I have purchased most of my supplies and equipment from the following sources:

Universal Wirecraft Company
P.O. Box 20206
Bradenton, FL 34203-0206
813/745-1219

JEMCO
3100 East Ridge Road
Lake Station, IN 46405
219/962-5870

Hoover & Strong
10700 Trade Rd.
Richmond, VA 23236
800-759-9997

A.F. Euro Tool
c/o Your Local Dealer

These businesses offer extremely fair prices and prompt service. Their integrity is above question.